CORONEL
and
THE FALKLANDS

CORONEL
and
THE FALKLANDS

GEOFFREY BENNETT

LONDON
B. T. BATSFORD LTD

By the same Author
BY HUMAN ERROR

First published 1962

© GEOFFREY BENNETT, 1962

MADE AND PRINTED IN GREAT BRITAIN BY
WILLIAM CLOWES AND SONS LTD, LONDON AND BECCLES
FOR THE PUBLISHERS
B. T. BATSFORD LTD
4 FITZHARDINGE STREET, PORTMAN SQUARE, LONDON W.1

PREFACE

Within three months of the outbreak of the First World War the incomparable reputation which the Royal Navy had earned in the eighteenth and nineteenth centuries suffered a blow that was the more bitter because it was wholly unexpected; one of Britain's cruiser squadrons was decisively defeated by a superior force from the new-born German Navy. The scene of the action was off the coast of Chile, half the world away from Plymouth, Portsmouth and the Nore, but the Admiralty reacted with such vigour that within six weeks the disaster was avenged; reinforcements sailed from Scapa Flow to the Falkland Islands, nearly 10,000 miles, and sent the victorious German force to the bottom of the South Atlantic. This dramatic reversal of the fortunes of war explains why more books, many with the interest inherent in participants' accounts, have been published about the Battles of Coronel and Falklands than about any other naval action, those between major fleets excepted.

In this new account, however, I have attempted the first comprehensive study to be written since the British and German official histories were compiled nearly forty years ago by authors who could not tap all the sources now open to the historian. In the words of Gilbert White: 'These observations are, I trust, true on the whole, though I do not pretend to show that they are perfectly void of mistake, or that a more nice observer might not make many additions since subjects of this kind are inexhaustible.' Nor can I 'pretend' that 'these observations' are wholly objective; that is more than can be expected of a writer who belongs to one of the participating nations; inevitably I have been conditioned by the British viewpoint; moreover I have been able to consult a larger number of British sources. Nonetheless, I have done my best to fulfil the historian's duty of being fair to both sides, withholding from neither such admiration and criticism as each seems to warrant. For history cannot be written without criticism, any more than an omelette can be made without breaking eggs. But this is no excuse for the denigration of British and German leaders of the First World War which is now the fashion; they had their merits or they would not have attained high rank. 'Nothing extenuate, nor set down aught in malice': I have highlighted achievements as well as pointed mistakes; remembering, for example, that, whilst Churchill's denial of responsibility for the British defeat at Coronel was unjust to Cradock, he also displayed the qualities of genius which were to earn for him a unique place in history 30 years later; that, despite Fisher's shabby treatment of Sturdee after his victory at the Falklands, he did more than any other man to prepare the Royal Navy for the First World War; and that, though von Spee's dilatory progress after Coronel and his decision to attack the Falklands combined to bring about the destruction of the German East Asiatic Squadron, its voyage across the Pacific which culminated in Cradock's defeat is as much to the German admiral's credit as the gallant way he fought and died.

London, 1962   GEOFFREY BENNETT

CONTENTS

ACKNOWLEDGMENT

This book is based chiefly on the British and German Admiralty records, including the *original* reports of the admirals and captains concerned (as first published these suffered some degree of censorship), and the British and German official histories, supplemented by the other published works and unpublished sources listed in the Bibliography.

My foremost debt is to two officers: Rear-Admiral S. P. Start has enabled me to reveal for the first time the truth about the *Canopus*'s speed and the reliability of her machinery, concerning which her captain's official reports contain so many contradictory statements that it is not surprising that the Official Historian was led into error; and Commander W. D. M. Stavely has kindly allowed me access to the collection of papers left by his grandfather, Admiral of the Fleet Sir Doveton Sturdee, whence I have been able to throw new light on, in particular, the manner in which he was relieved of his appointment as Chief of Staff at the Admiralty after Coronel, and his spiteful treatment by Lord Fisher following the Falklands victory.

For personal recollections and for the loan of letters, diaries and journals (whose keeping by officers serving afloat was not forbidden for security reasons until 1915), which have enabled me to add flesh to the bare bones of the official records, I have to thank the following, many of whom played some part in these stirring events: Admirals of the Fleet Earl Mountbatten of Burma and Sir Henry Oliver, Admirals H. E. Dannreuther, Sir David Luce and H. A. B. Wollaston, Vice-Admirals J. W. Carrington and R. D. Oliver, Rear-Admirals M. G. Bennett, B. L. G. Sebastian and Sir Lionel Sturdee, Captains T. H. Back, J. S. Bethell, G. D. Campbell, A. D. Duckworth, H. E. M. Spencer-Cooper, R. C. Steele and R. R. Stewart, Commanders H. H-G. Begbie, Lloyd Hirst, L. I. G. Leveson, R. H. Mandley, P. J. M. Penney, R. C. T. Rowe, M. G. Saunders, D. A. Stride and R. T. Young, and Mr. Richard Middlemas. For other help I have to thank Lieutenant-Commander P. K. Kemp and the staff of the Admiralty Library, the staffs of the Imperial War Museum, National Maritime Museum, Public Record Office, Royal United Service Institution and Westminster Central Reference Libraries, and of the Federal German Armed Forces Historical Research Office, the Captain of H.M.S. *Excellent*, the Dean of York Minster and the Vicar of Catherington Church, near Portsmouth.

Grateful acknowledgements are due to the authors and publishers of the many works from which I have quoted, especially to The Controller, H.M. Stationery Office (*Naval Staff Monographs, OU.5413 and OU.5413C*, which are crown copyright), Commander Lloyd Hirst (*Coronel and After*), Sir Winston Churchill, Messrs Macmillan and Charles Scribner's Sons (*The World Crisis, 1911–1918*), Professor Arthur Marder and Messrs Cape (*Fear God and Dread Nought*, and *Portrait of an Admiral*) and Messrs W. L. Wylie and M. F. Wren and Messrs Cassell (*Sea Fights of the Great War*).

Finally, but not for the first time, I have to record my thanks to Miss Adrienne Edye and Miss Margaret Dyson for typing and retyping my manuscript, and to both my father and my wife for reading and checking it. Without so much assistance this book could not have been produced; responsibility for the result is, nonetheless, wholly mine.

8

LIST OF ILLUSTRATIONS

The Author and Publishers wish to thank the following for permission to reproduce the illustrations.

Captain A. D. Duckworth, R.N., for fig. 32

The Imperial War Museum for figs. 4, 5, 7, 9–11, 14, 15, 24, 25, 27, 28, 30, 33 and 34

The Director and Trustees of the National Maritime Museum, Greenwich, for figs. 8, 23 and 29

The National Portrait Gallery for fig. 18

Odhams Press Ltd for fig. 22 (from Winston Churchill, *The World Crisis*)

Radio Times Hulton Picture Library for figs. 16 and 17

Süddeutscher Verlag, Munich, for figs. 3, 13, 19–21, 31 and 35

Part one

CORONEL

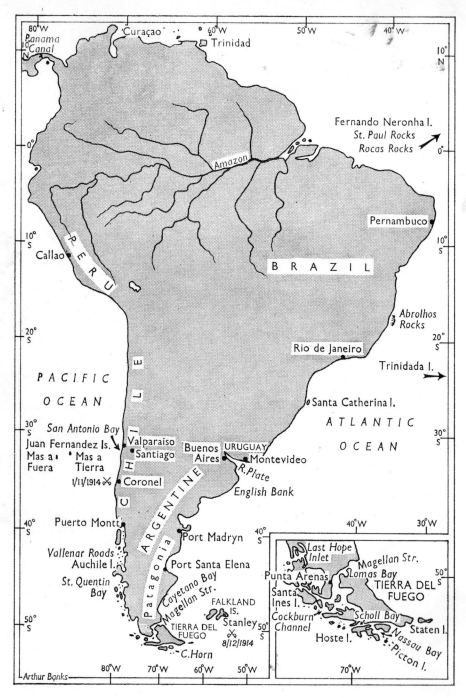

1 *Map of South America*

I

1st November 1914

'As we stepped aboard [H.M.S. *Monmouth*] I heard a Marine
say: "Here's some more poor little chaps being sent to be
killed." If I had only known that we were the only ones that
were to be saved from that ill-fated ship. . . .'

From the Diary of Naval Cadet Mandley*

'A HEAVING unsettled sea, and away over to the western horizon an
angry yellow sun is setting clearly below a forbidding bank of the
blackest of wind-charged clouds. In the centre of the picture lies an
immense solitary cruiser with a flag . . . at her masthead blowing out
broad and clear from the first rude kiss given by the fast rising breeze.
Then, away from half the points of the compass, are seen the swift ships
of a cruiser squadron all drawing in to join their flagship. Some are
close, others far distant and hull down, with nothing but their fitful
smoke against the fast fading lighted sky to mark their whereabouts;
but like wild ducks at evening flighting home to some well-known spot,
so are they, with one desire, hurrying back at the behest of their mother-
ship to gather round her for the night.' The quotation, with its poetic
feeling for words, comes from Rear-Admiral Sir Christopher Cradock's
Whispers from the Fleet, written when he was a captain in command of
H.M. Ships *Leviathan* and *Swiftsure* in the first days of the dreadnought
era. But such a description might well have been included in his dispatch reporting the events of 1st November, 1914, if he had survived
the disaster which overwhelmed his squadron that Sunday evening off
Coronel.

Today there may be little of practical value in *Whispers from the Fleet*:
Cradock was concerned with reciprocating engines and coal-fired

---

* Mandley with nine other 15-year-old Dartmouth cadets joined the *Monmouth*
for passage to St Vincent, where, fortunately, they transferred to H.M.S. *Carnarvon*.

13

boilers, magnetic compasses and guns with nothing but the most elementary fire control; turbines and oil fuel were recent innovations, gyro compasses and director firing were yet to come, radar and guided missiles undreamed of. But to the student of history this book mirrors its author; and Cradock's personality is important to an understanding of the circumstances attending his defeat by Vice-Admiral Graf von Spee:

> A dash into a basin at twenty knots, even in the strongest of winds and cross tides, is unnecessary. Should it come off, there is only a matey or two to see; and if it does not, there is a stone wall and a court of enquiry ahead. . . .

> When a hammock is being used as a shroud, the last stitch of the sailmaker's needle is neatly popped through the tip of the nose, and then there *can* be no mistake. . . .

Cradock, whose photograph shows handsome features with the hint of a smile in the wide-set eyes, was a man of wit and wisdom, of sense and sensibility. Admiral of the Fleet Lord Cunningham remembers him 'as always being immaculately dressed, with a pointed, neatly trimmed dark beard, which reminded one of Sir Francis Drake'. The Elizabethan parallel fits his gay, debonair personality. He was a good mixer who enjoyed company; a bachelor who was far from being a misogynist. An officer who was with him in the *Good Hope* almost to the last recalls how he liked to leave the loneliness of his admiral's quarters and join the ship's officers in the wardroom for a drink before dinner. And the A.D.C. to the Governor of the Falkland Islands noted that Cradock and his dog 'would come wandering up to Government House every day for a yarn and a meal or else the Governor would go off to the *Good Hope*. . . . He was a dear old bloke and as keen as a terrier.'

Born in 1862, he had joined the old *Britannia*, in which he was later to serve as a commander, at the age of 13. As a lieutenant he saw more than sea service: he was with the naval brigade garrisoning Upper Egypt in 1884, and later with the Eastern Sudan field force at the occupation of Affatit and the battle of Toker, for which he received the first of the decorations that, by 1914, were a testimonial to a remarkable career. Time in the Royal Yacht brought him promotion; in 1900 he commanded the *Alacrity*, the admiral's yacht in China where the polo which he and his friends David Beatty (later Admiral of the Fleet Earl Beatty) and Roger Keyes (later Admiral of the Fleet Lord Keyes) enjoyed in Hong Kong was interrupted by the Boxer Rebellion in which all three officers distinguished themselves. Cradock served with the British naval brigade which led the Allied force at the storming of the Taku forts, of which he wrote in *Whispers from the Fleet*:

> Let me call to mind the goodly sight of those two destroyers *Fame* [commanded by Lieutenant Roger Keyes] and *Whiting* slipping through the black rushing waters of the Peiho at the opening of that furious and distracting midnight bombardment of the Taku forts, bound to attack and capture the Chinese destroyers and arsenal, knowing naught of what was ahead of them, and caring less.

Of Cradock's own courage, an officer who was with the British naval detachment recalled that

> at one point it was necessary for the [Allied] force to pass along a narrow bend in single file. A few Chinese snipers had discovered this, so that the spot was rather a 'windy corner'. The Germans . . . were holding us up and reluctant to go on. Cradock and Beatty arrived, both mounted, and were furious at the delay. Failing to goad the Germans into activity, they dismounted and led their horses up an incline, passing through the Germans. On reaching the top, they mounted again under a shower of whistling bullets and walked their horses down the other side. This was too much for us, and we became braver and scrambled over the Germans, carrying some of them with us.

As a captain in a series of sea commands, Cradock (to quote the *Dictionary of National Biography*) 'filled every appointment with credit to himself, and brought to his duties not only abounding energy but the sporting instinct. . . . [For him] the strength of the Navy consisted in the complete loyalty and good comradeship between officers and men and "the sacred laws of naval discipline". To him the Navy was not a collection of ships, but a community of men with high purpose.' Since the First Sea Lord, Admiral of the Fleet Lord Fisher, considered him 'one of our very best officers' it is not surprising that he achieved the rank of rear-admiral in 1910.

A year later Cradock had a chance to show both his courage and his seaman's skill. He had initial charge of the rescue operations when the P. & O. liner *Delhi*, whose passengers included the Duke of Fife and the Princess Royal and their family, was wrecked on the coast of Morocco. His C.-in-C., Jellicoe (later Admiral of the Fleet Earl Jellicoe), wrote that 'at about noon Admiral Cradock got the Royal party and a few others into one . . . of our cutters. . . . They swamped close to the shore but the party were all got safely on the beach though wet through and only half clad.' For this Cradock was made a K.C.V.O. His last appointment followed; at the age of 51 he went to command the North America and West Indies Station, where for 18 months he enjoyed himself acting as an ambassador for Britain on the best of all the Royal Navy's stations in time of peace. But then came war, and circumstances to be related later took him down round Cape Horn to the coast of Chile. 'We hear', wrote an officer in the *Glasgow*, 'Admiral Cradock is coming south to our station. . . . He has always been in any naval fighting during the past thirty years, so he may run the show well.'

Cradock was, in sum, a gallant gentleman, a most likeable leader of men who had made his own particular niche in a Service for whose spirit and traditions he had a strong affection, and a skilled seaman who had had his baptism of fire and proved his courage, yet possessed the sensitivity, the special temperament of the artist. And these characteristics account for his defeat at Coronel, for all the short-comings of the Admiralty in London which led him to disaster.

The 'immense solitary cruiser with [Cradock's] flag at her masthead blowing out broad and clear' over the storm-swept scene with which this chapter opened was H.M.S. *Good Hope*. Completed in 1902 with a designed speed of 23 knots, she was a well protected vessel displacing 14,100 tons, albeit undergunned for the great size of her hull: she was armed with two 9·2-inch and sixteen 6-inch guns. On paper she might be only half-way through her useful life; in fact she was as obsolete as a pre-dreadnought battleship. Her big guns might be mounted in centre-line turrets, but her 6-inch were arranged in broadside batteries. Fisher realised this weakness: 'Guns . . . on the main deck . . . are practically useless. We know this from experience. Half the time they cannot see the object for want of view . . . and the other half they are flooded out by the sea.' So, with other armoured cruisers of her era, she had been reduced to Third Fleet status before 'Armageddon'.

'To merely hustle a complement of the required ratings into a ship is not to make her a really efficient fighting machine. The key stone of our preparedness for war has . . . to be inserted, namely the provision of efficient nucleus [active service] crews.' But Fisher's dictum only applied to the Second Fleet: on mobilisation Captain Francklin had to commission the *Good Hope* with a crew including more than 90 per cent Reservists who could not immediately turn her into 'a really efficient fighting machine'. Yet this was assumed, as with many another vessel: the *Good Hope* was given no opportunity to train her officers and men in their duties in action. She steamed out of Portsmouth harbour on Sunday, 2nd August, as the Salvation Army band on Gosport Hard

2 *Vice-Admiral Maximilian Graf von Spee, commander of the German East Asiatic Squadron at the battles of Coronel and the Falklands*

3 *Rear-Admiral Sir Christopher Cradock, commander of the British force at the battle of Coronel*

4   *The British armoured cruiser* Monmouth *which was sunk at Coronel*

5   *Cradock's ill-fated flagship at Coronel, the armoured cruiser* Good Hope

played *Nearer My God to Thee*; and she went straight across to Halifax. There Cradock transferred his flag to her, and she was employed continuously in the western Atlantic, down to the Pernambuco area and later to the Falkland Islands, protecting British shipping against marauding German cruisers. By 1st November, 1914, her company might be inspired by a spirit of death or glory, but in the three months since the outbreak of war they had carried out only one full-calibre firing. 'It certainly is the limit', wrote the *Glasgow*'s gunnery officer, 'taking a ship like that off the dockyard wall, giving her four rounds of practice [shell] a gun and then putting her up against a ship like [the *Scharnhorst*].'

The 'ships of [Cradock's] squadron all drawing in to join their flagship' numbered four, of whom only one merited the adjective 'swift'. The largest was the *Monmouth* of 9,800 tons, an armoured cruiser completed a year later than the *Good Hope* with whom she shared more than one deficiency.

> I was snotty of the watch going rounds. It was a roughish night but nothing very bad with the wind on the starboard bow. When I got to A2 starboard forward main deck gun [the crew] asked if they could shut the gun ports, open for night defence stations, as they were being washed out. I conveyed the request to the bridge where the information was received with considerable surprise.

In a seaway the *Monmouth*'s effective broadside was only nine 6-inch guns; for unlike the *Good Hope*'s these were not supported by heavier weapons: 'Sir William White designed the "County" class but forgot the guns' was Fisher's acid criticism. 'She was practically condemned as unfit for further service', wrote one of the *Carnarvon*'s midshipmen, 'but was hauled off the dockyard wall [and] commissioned with a scratch crew' under Captain Brandt and sent to patrol Britain's trade routes, with no opportunity to train her company to fight their ship against a determined foe.

The 'swift' ship was the *Glasgow*, of 25 knots. Completed as recently as 1911, she had been in commission under the command of Captain Luce for more than two years before the war, Britain's only warship in South American waters, so that she was an efficient fighting unit. But she was only a light cruiser, without armour, of 4,800 tons, with two 6-inch and ten 4-inch guns—Fisher's concept of a vessel whose purpose was to scout for the battlefleet, to fight the enemy's light forces to obtain it, but to seek safety in flight from more powerful units. Whilst the *Otranto*, Captain Edwards, was no more than a 12,000-ton liner equipped for war with eight 4·7-inch guns, one of many auxiliaries which the Navy needed to protect British shipping against attacks by similar vessels, not to fight enemy warships.

The fifth of Cradock's vessels was the battleship *Canopus*. Her pre-dreadnought vintage was of small importance in waters where there was no other battleship, no enemy vessel with 12-inch guns to match the four she mounted, together with twelve 6-inch, on an armoured hull that displaced 12,950 tons. But she had aged since completion in 1899: when paid off into the Third Fleet in 1912 she could only raise four-fifths of her designed horse-power. Intended for scrapping in 1915, she had been hurriedly commissioned in August, 1914, with a crew of reservists under the command of Captain Heathcote Grant, and, after a few weeks escorting the Expeditionary Force across the Channel, ordered to the Falklands. And since she had carried out no practice full-calibre firings, her gunnery (though the enemy could not know this) must have been of a very low standard.

These five vessels, of which only one was fit to fight a well-trained foe, were the only British ships off the west coast of South America on 1st November, 1914; and they were not concentrated. The *Monmouth* and *Glasgow* were with the flagship, but the fourth ship in company with the *Good Hope* was the *Otranto*, not the *Canopus*. When temporarily commissioned for the Spithead Review in July, 1914, a three-hours, full-power trial had proved the old battleship's maximum speed to be 17 knots. But when she reached the Falklands in the latter part of October, her engineer commander reported that her condensers were so faulty that she could not do more than 12 knots. Grant, who had no reason to doubt his principal technical adviser, told Cradock this when the *Canopus* and *Good Hope* were in company for a few hours on 22nd October. And the admiral had no alternative to believing this limitation, any more than Whitehall when he informed them of it. She was, it seemed,

> *A fortress yet: but island more than ship*
> *Whose niggardly twelve knots retard the rest.*

The British admiral knew the strength of the German force off the west coast of South America. On 5th October the Admiralty had signalled him: 'It appears that *Scharnhorst* and *Gneisenau* are working across [the Pacific] to South America. You must be prepared to meet them in company, possibly with a *Dresden* scouting for them'; to which

Cradock replied on the 8th: 'Indications show possibility of *Dresden*, *Leipzig*, *Nürnberg* joining *Gneisenau* and *Scharnhorst*.' The two ships Cradock might 'meet in company' were sister cruisers completed five years later than the *Good Hope*, with armour similar to hers, though their speed was limited to 20 knots, so that their tonnage had been kept down to 11,600. But each mounted eight 8·2-inch and six 5·9-inch guns, so arranged that even in bad weather they could fight a broadside of six 8·2-inch plus three 5·9-inch. Moreover, their crews were highly trained: both the *Scharnhorst*, Captain Schultz, and the *Gneisenau*, Captain Maerker, had been long in commission as the principal units of Germany's East Asiatic Squadron, based before the war on Tsingtau where they had achieved distinction for their gunnery efficiency: indeed, the *Scharnhorst* had won the Kaiser's prize two years running. So, except for their speed, these two ships were measurably superior to the *Good Hope* and *Monmouth*. The *Dresden*, Captain Lüdecke, the *Leipzig*, Captain Haun, and the *Nürnberg*, Captain von Schönberg, were light cruisers of 3,250–3,600 tons, completed 1906–09. They, too, had been commissioned before the war and could be compared with the *Glasgow* except for their armament: they mounted ten 4·1-inch guns apiece, five to a broadside, whereas the British vessel could bring two 6-inch as well as five 4-inch to bear on the beam. And each, of course, was more than a match for the *Otranto*, not least by virtue of a margin of 6 knots speed.*

Unless, therefore, Cradock had the *Canopus* with his squadron, he ran the risk of meeting a German force superior to his own. But he believed his purpose to be the location and destruction of the enemy, and there was small chance of the enemy accepting action with a battleship; having greater speed they could always avoid her. Moreover Cradock might locate one or more enemy ships weaker than his own three cruisers, when he should be able to bring them to action and sink them before they could be reinforced. As important, if he was to find the enemy at all in an area so vast, with so many uninhabited bays and islands, he needed both speed and ships. And the *Otranto* only reduced the British squadron to 18 knots, whilst Fisher had written: 'Large mercantile vessels are the best scouts', in which capacity they had proved their worth in the Russo-Japanese war. Cradock had put the matter succinctly in a signal to the Admiralty as recently as 27th October: 'With reference to [Admiralty orders] to search for enemy and our great desire for early success, consider it impracticable on

* For a concise summary of the details of the British and German ships, see Appendix I.

account of *Canopus*'s slow speed, to find and destroy enemy's squadron.
. . . *Canopus* will be employed . . . convoying colliers. . . .' So on 1st
November the old battleship was some 300 miles astern of the rest of
the British force.

The commander of the German squadron, with his flag in the
Scharnhorst, was Maximilian Graf von Spee. Born in Copenhagen, he
had entered the navy at the age of 16, dividing his time as a junior
officer between training establishments at Kiel and foreign service in
ships off the African coasts, and as Port Commander in the Cameroons.
He was invalided from this last appointment with a severe fever which
left a legacy of rheumatism from which he sometimes suffered considerably. By 1893 he had become a gunnery specialist, serving in the
pre-dreadnought *Bayern* and as adjutant to the Superintendent of
Coastal Artillery, after which he was on Rear-Admiral Prince Henry of
Prussia's staff during the China War. Promoted commander in 1899, he
was executive officer of the battleship *Brandenburg* for two years, and in
the weapon department of the German Admiralty for three. As a
captain he commanded the cruiser *Wittelsbach* and was Chief of Staff to
the Admiral, North Sea Station at Wilhelmshaven.

Riding high on the wave of the German Navy's rapid growth in the
first decade of the twentieth century, von Spee thus reached flag rank in
1910 at the early age of 49 and hoisted his flag in the cruiser *Yorck* as
second-in-command of the High Seas Fleet's Scouting Groups. Then,
after a period of special duty at the Kiel headquarters of the Commander-in-Chief, Baltic, he was given his most challenging appointment, command of Germany's East Asiatic Squadron, where he was
promoted vice-admiral in November, 1913. Thus, by 1914 he had
added to 35 years' varied service in the Imperial German Navy the
advantage of two years' knowledge of the area in which he would have
to operate his ships in war.

He was tall, broad-shouldered and strongly built, with a pointed
beard that concealed a square chin, and blue eyes which sometimes had
a serene, almost pious look, at others flashed with the sharp severity of
lightning. Combined with a jerky manner, this last facet of his appearance was in keeping with the aggressive aspect of his personality. His
keen intelligence, his fighting spirit, his strength of will, his willingness
to take responsibility, and his confidence in the training and spirit of his
men, all made him a dangerous adversary. But he was far from being the
common British concept of a Hun; coming from an aristocratic family,
he was at all times a true gentleman. A Catholic and happily married,

he had a warm humanity, a sense of fair play that endeared him to his subordinates; and he shared with Cradock the fatalistic outlook characteristic of many seamen, perhaps by virtue of their calling: 'These men see the works of the Lord and his wonders in the deep.' Amongst the components of von Spee's character, serenity was of importance to the success with which, during the first four months of the war, he conducted operations half the world away from Germany, hunted by ever-growing Allied forces, without a base, wholly dependent on a tenuous life-line of supply ships for coal and stores. But another component, aggressiveness, is more important when considering the circumstances which led him to engage Cradock off Coronel, and another British squadron six weeks later off the Falkland Islands.

This, then, was the man in command of the ships for which the British force was searching, of which Cradock had had no definite information since the first week in October when the Admiralty signalled: '*Scharnhorst* on the way between Marquesas and Easter Island', and he himself visited Orange Bay and found evidence that the *Dresden* had been there on 11th September. So he could not know whether von Spee was making for Cape Horn or the Panama Canal: either was possible, but 4,000 miles of Pacific water separated them. He had therefore brought his squadron as far north as Vallenar Roads by 29th October where he established a coaling base in the shadow of Mount Isquiliac. And that afternoon the *Glasgow*, which had been sent ahead to reconnoitre the coast, to locate a German sailing vessel said to be making for Santa Maria Island, and to go into Coronel to send and receive signals,* intercepted a number of wireless messages in cipher which she identified as coming from a German transmitter no more than 150 miles away. Receiving this important news early on the 30th—the first positive evidence that a German warship was near at hand—Cradock sailed at 0600† with the *Good Hope* and *Monmouth* and headed north, keeping out of sight of the Chilean coast. He left orders for the *Canopus*, which entered the roadstead shortly afterwards, to follow with his two colliers when she had coaled and repaired a reported engine defect.

* The need to do this is explained in Appendix II where other relevant information concerning signal communications will be found.

† Although not then adopted by the Royal Navy, the 24-hour clock is used in this book since it avoids the need to refer to a.m. and p.m. In all quotations times have been altered accordingly; and whenever necessary to avoid confusion, times given in German reports have been adjusted to conform with the British which were four and a half hours behind G.M.T.

Grant now learned that his engineer commander was a sick man, that the strain of war had undermined the health of his principal technical adviser so as to lead him to magnify the difficulties of maintaining the ageing battleship's machinery and of firing her Belleville boilers with a scratch crew of stokers. The *Canopus* was, in fact, suffering from no more than a leaking piston-rod gland which could have been repaired at any time; more important she was still capable of steaming at $16\frac{1}{2}$ knots, as was shortly to be proved. The first point was immaterial since the ship needed coal, thus giving the few hours required to deal with the piston-rod gland. But Cradock could only be informed by wireless that the *Canopus* could still achieve a speed near to that for which she had been designed; and Grant did not consider this justified since he did not believe the admiral would delay his northward progress so that the battleship could catch up with his faster cruisers.

Whether Cradock would have kept the *Canopus* with him if he had not been so seriously misled by the failure of the health of a single man into believing that she was too slow for his purpose, before he left the Falklands to steam round into the Pacific, can only be conjectured. On balance, from what one knows of Cradock, one doubts it, so that this side-light on history did not, perhaps, affect its course.

Next day, the 31st, the *Good Hope* was joined by the *Otranto* which had been visiting Puerto Montt, for intelligence which the pro-German community declined to provide. And that same morning the *Glasgow* heard further Telefunken transmissions closer than before, and identified the *Leipzig*'s call-sign: apparently the German light cruiser was communicating with a merchant ship. Cradock responded by ordering Luce to hasten his visit to Coronel, and to sail again in time to rendezvous with the *Good Hope* at 1200 next day, 50 miles to the west of Coronel.

The 1st November dawned fine and clear, except for patches of fog which were soon cleared by a south-easterly wind that tempered the warmth of an early summer day. Indeed, the wind was strong enough to raise a sea that made boatwork impossible when the *Glasgow* joined, so that the signals she brought from the Admiralty had to be transferred in a small cask towed across the flagship's bows. Luce could give Cradock no other news; but the interception of further transmissions from the *Leipzig* at 1350 confirmed the admiral's opinion that there was only a single German warship in the vicinity and that he could expect to meet her soon. So he ordered his squadron to form on a line of search NE by E, 15 miles apart, in the order *Good Hope*, *Monmouth*, *Otranto* and

Glasgow (nearest the coast) and steamed NW by N at a speed of 15 knots. But the line of ships running before the wind, which now approached gale force, was not fully extended by 1620 when Luce sighted smoke on his starboard bow and altered course towards it.

The *Leipzig* was not alone that afternoon off Coronel: von Spee was there with his whole force, two armoured cruisers and three light cruisers. Early in September, when the *Scharnhorst* and *Gneisenau* were in the western Pacific, he had decided on the Cape Horn route to the Atlantic, later intelligence confirming the wisdom of his choice. German agents in South America told him that, whilst there were indications of a strong Anglo-Japanese force concentrating off the west coast of North America, he had little to fear off the Chilean sea-board, or to the immediate east of Cape Horn, if he kept his force together. And 24 hours after leaving the isolated Mas a Fuera island, where his ships coaled on 27th October, von Spee knew from his agents ashore that there was only Cradock's squadron off the Chilean coast. Moreover, intercepted wireless traffic suggested that his own deceptive use of the *Leipzig*'s transmitter had been successful, and that the British ships were separated and acting independently in the protection of trade, unaware that so strong a German squadron was in the area. So, on the 29th, he ordered his ships to close Valparaiso where the local authorities were making difficulties about one of his supply vessels leaving harbour, after which he intended to proceed south along the coast, his aim being the destruction of Cradock's force.

Consequently von Spee was to the south of Valparaiso at 0250 on 1st November when he received a momentous message from the supply ship *Göttingen*, which he had sent into Coronel: 'British light cruiser anchored in Coronel Roads at 1900 on 31st October.' Realising that International Law would require the *Glasgow* to leave within 24 hours, the German admiral disposed his force to catch her. The *Scharnhorst* and the light cruisers were to guard the northern entrance between Santa Maria and Coronel, the *Gneisenau* was to watch the Boca Chica, whilst, if necessary, one light cruiser was to enter Coronel at 1800 to ensure that the Chilean authorities adhered to the 24-hour rule. This disposition, coupled with the need to intercept several merchant vessels, resulted in the German warships being somewhat scattered: late in the afternoon the *Nürnberg* was out of sight to the north-east, while the *Dresden* was about 12 miles astern of the rest of von Spee's force which was 40 miles north of Aranco Bay. All were unaware that the *Glasgow* had, most fortunately for her, already left Coronel that morning.

> It was a beautiful day, the sea was of a dark green colour, the crests of the waves were tipped with white foam which glistened in the sunlight. In a cloudless sky the sun was slowly sinking to rest. A stiff breeze had been blowing since noon. It came from the south with a force of six. As the [German] cruiser squadron was proceeding on a southerly course, wind and sea came from starboard. The big ships began to roll and the small cruisers shipped water.

Such were the conditions when, shortly after 1630, the *Leipzig* sighted smoke and hauled out to starboard to investigate.

Thus, when the two squadrons first made contact, each admiral was unaware that he would meet the other's squadron; each supposed he was about to encounter and overwhelm a single light cruiser. This impression was initially sustained by the coincidence that the *Leipzig*, the single light cruiser that Cradock expected to catch, was the first to be sighted by the British force, whilst the *Glasgow*, the single light cruiser that von Spee hoped to trap in Coronel, was the first to be sighted by the German squadron. But the similarity ends there: though the difference in numbers between the two forces might be no more than two light cruisers to von Spee's advantage, there was a great disparity in their armaments. In addition to the efficiency of the German guns' crews, the effective weight of their ships' broadside fire was nearly double that of the British, chiefly due to the larger number of big-calibre guns carried by the German heavy cruisers.

At 1640 Luce, investigating a tell-tale smudge of smoke on the horizon as he had so often done before in the past three months, sighted and identified the enemy. Both the *Otranto*, next in Cradock's line of search, and the *Monmouth* beyond her to seaward, moved to the *Glasgow*'s support so that the *Monmouth* lost sight of the *Good Hope*. But, as Luce swung his plunging ship around towards the flagship's position and rang for full speed on the *Glasgow*'s engines, he was able to span the distance of more than 50 miles that separated him from Cradock with the wireless news that he had sighted more than the *Leipzig*; the *Scharnhorst* and *Gneisenau* were in company with her. We may picture Cradock standing with Captain Francklin on the *Good Hope*'s bridge as his flag lieutenant showed him Luce's message. Among the three rows of medal ribbons on the left breast of his monkey jacket, one is stained with ink. 'That ribbon', he had told the Governor's A.D.C. at Port

Stanley only a fortnight before, 'belongs to the First Class Order of the Blue Ape, or something, that the Kaiser gave me. I couldn't tear it off without ruining all the others; so I got an ink bottle and made it look as unpleasant as possible. I wish I had the medal or cross, or whatever it was, here; I'd kick the damned thing into the scuppers.' So there can be no doubt of his reaction to the news that he had, unexpectedly, run into a superior enemy force. 'It was as I thought', wrote Lieutenant-Commander Verner, who as gunnery officer of the *Inflexible* was to play a part in avenging Cradock's death. 'An English admiral, manœuvred into a hopeless position from which he *could* have extricated himself, refused to do so because "he would rather burst than let a damned scoundrel of a German, etc.".' (The quotation is adapted from one of Nelson's observations: 'I would rather burst than let a damned rascal of a Frenchman know that peace or war affected me with either joy or sorrow.')

Cradock could have ordered an immediate alteration of course to the south and escaped. He had plenty of sea room; von Spee could not know that the two British armoured cruisers were so near; moreover, the Germans had steam for only 14 knots. Even when the *Scharnhorst* and *Gneisenau* had worked up to full speed, the British ships would have the advantage of a couple of knots over their opponents—except for the *Otranto*, and she had every chance of escaping under the cover of night since sunset was so near. Moreover, Cradock would have been acting in full accord with the instructions he had received from the Admiralty had he decided to fall back on the *Canopus*, steaming slowly northwards with the two colliers she was escorting some 300 miles to the south. But from all that we know it is impossible to accept that any such idea crossed Cradock's mind that afternoon. It would have been the complete negation of his aim to seek out and destroy the enemy; once he lost touch with von Spee, for whom Britain and her Allies in the Pacific had been searching for so long, who could tell when he would be so fortunate as to find him again. More important, avoiding action with the enemy was no more within Cradock's conception than it had been in Sir Richard Grenville's 'at Flores in the Azores' or was to be in Captain Warburton-Lee's at Narvik in 1940. Flight is the antithesis of the British naval tradition; there have been so many occasions when a numerically inferior British force has not hesitated to engage a stronger enemy. Moreover, it was not necessary to sink von Spee's ships; lacking a repair base outside distant European waters, damage would reduce them to impotence and force them to seek internment in a neutral port.

Having chosen battle, Cradock selected the best course open to him when only a short period of daylight remained in an era when ships of the Royal Navy were not equipped for night fighting; he decided to force an action with von Spee. At 1700 he ordered his ships to concentrate on the *Glasgow* which was nearest the enemy; and by turning the *Good Hope* to the east, where his other three ships were already headed W by S to join him, he was able to form his squadron in single line ahead in the order *Good Hope, Monmouth, Glasgow* and *Otranto* on a south-easterly course three-quarters of an hour later. This was intended to bring them quickly within 6-inch gun range of von Spee, since these weapons were the British ships' principal armament, but it headed them into a sea that made the *Good Hope*'s and *Monmouth*'s main deck untenable.

Cradock's decision to include the *Otranto* in the line is difficult to understand: before contact she had proved her value in prolonging his line of search 15 miles, but she could not fight enemy cruisers: 'We all thought he would leave the *Otranto*', wrote the *Glasgow*'s gunnery officer, '[but perhaps] he did not like leaving [her] to look after herself . . . [she] is such an enormous hulk she can be seen for miles on the darkest night.' He should have ordered her clear to the west, especially since, so far as he knew, von Spee's force was limited to three ships, none of which could be released to pursue an armed liner. As it was, Cradock not only kept the *Otranto* with him but tempered his desire to close the enemy with concern for her safety: as late as 1850 he signalled his force: 'I cannot go down and engage the enemy at present leaving *Otranto*.'

Meanwhile the *Leipzig* identified the *Glasgow* and *Monmouth* at 1647 and eight minutes later recognised the *Otranto*. Von Spee no more hesitated than Cradock had done: ordering the *Nürnberg* and *Dresden* to join him, he 'steamed at full speed in pursuit, keeping the enemy four points to starboard. The wind was south, force six, with a correspondingly high sea, so that I had to be careful not to be manoeuvred into a lee position. Moreover, the course chosen helped to cut off the enemy from the neutral coast.' Von Spee's decision needs no examination such as has been given to Cradock's; unless he should discover that the *Canopus* was close at hand, when he could use his superior speed to avoid her, action with a force clearly inferior to his own was his only course in the light of his already mentioned aim, to destroy the enemy's ships off the west coast of South America. To quote a German authority:

Scharnhorst hoisted a flag signal: 'Pursue the enemy. Full speed ahead.' As the flags were lowered the leading ship turned to starboard towards the enemy. The water broke foaming over their bows as the vessels turned and raced on over the sea . . . it surged right over their fore-castles. The German ships shuddered under the heavy thudding of their engines. The smoke poured out of their funnels in thick heavy swathes and streamed behind the squadron. . . . The admiral dreaded the night which would provide cover for the enemy. It was terrible to think that he might escape. . . . The minutes flew by one after another. They were but slowly gaining on the enemy. The wild chase had already lasted over an hour. At 1750 a fresh vessel was sighted. She proved to be the *Good Hope* [and] placed herself at the head of the English line. . . . The two squadrons were approaching each other on a southerly parallel course and their battle ensigns were hoisted on their masts. Just as the sun was sinking in a blood-red flame of fire, the fight began.

At 1804 'the British squadron turned (together) four points towards the enemy, with a view to closing them and forcing them to action before sunset', wrote the *Glasgow*'s navigating officer. 'If successful, [this] would have put them at a great disadvantage, owing to the British squadron being between the enemy and the sun.' But von Spee realised the danger of having his gunlayers blinded by the sun's glare; he turned away. So Cradock resumed his southerly course at *Otranto*'s best speed in a head sea of 16 knots. And at 1818 he wirelessed the *Canopus*: 'I am now going to attack the enemy', to which the battleship replied with her position, 250 miles away. The distance between the two forces was still some two miles beyond the extreme range of their heavy guns, and only closing slowly; for von Spee, who had been joined by the *Dresden*, while the *Nürnberg* was still hull down to the north, was waiting until, from the British point of view, the sun

> dipped below the horizon shortly before 1900 when [wrote one of the *Glasgow*'s officers] we were silhouetted against the afterglow with a clear horizon behind us to show up splashes from falling shells while the (German) ships were smudged into low black shapes scarcely discernible against the background of gathering darkness. Ranges became increasingly difficult to take; the enemy were no longer avoiding action. . . .

At 1900, when the range was down to 12,300 yards, von Spee signalled his ships to open fire.

> And with that [order—to quote a German source] disaster broke over Admiral Cradock's squadron. Barely three seconds afterwards the very air quivered under the thunderous crash of [the *Scharnhorst*'s first] salvo. A light brown powder smoke blew past the ship to be carried rapidly

away by the strong breeze. The fire zone was clear. The ships of the enemy's line lay like so many dark shadows sharply silhouetted against the red gold evening sky.

Disaster, indeed, it was; the Germans had more than the advantage of the light; initially the British were within range of 12 of the enemy's 8·2-inch guns to which only the *Good Hope*'s two 9·2-inch could reply. Thus, in the words of the British First Lord, 'began the saddest naval action in the war. Of the officers and men in both squadrons that faced each other in these strong seas so far from home, nine out of ten were doomed to perish. The British were to die that night. . . .'

'Immediately after the *Scharnhorst* . . . the *Dresden* opened fire on the *Otranto*. [The German light cruiser's] first salvoes were successful', wrote a German officer. 'The English auxiliary . . . turned off and made for the open sea.' At least a quarter of an hour before this the *Otranto*'s captain, seeing that his ship could play no useful part in the action that was imminent, had signalled Cradock suggesting he should keep out of range. But the only reply he received from the *Good Hope* was a message that was never finished: 'There is danger; proceed at your utmost speed. . . .' Perhaps Cradock intended Edwards should escape, but since he had not been detached earlier, the *Otranto*'s captain decided that the admiral wished his fledgling warship to remain under the protective wing of his heavy cruisers. So, when the *Gneisenau* put two shells over his bridge, one salvo 50 yards on his starboard bow and another 150 yards astern, to none of which he could reply, Edwards edged out of the line to starboard and conformed with the flagship's southerly course beyond range of the enemy's guns.

The *Leipzig*'s initial salvo fell far short of the *Glasgow*, and her fire remained ineffective for nearly 10 minutes: the range was too great for her 4·1-inch guns. But the *Gneisenau*'s and *Scharnhorst*'s shooting was excellent from the start; their first salvoes were very close to the *Good Hope* and *Monmouth*, notwithstanding heavy rolling, and the *Scharnhorst*'s third salvo put the *Good Hope*'s forward 9·2-inch gun out of action, whilst the *Gneisenau*'s struck the *Monmouth*'s forecastle, destroying her foremost turret and setting her on fire. Before this, however, the British ships had opened fire on the enemy, the *Good Hope* at the *Scharnhorst*, the *Monmouth* at the *Gneisenau*, and a little later the *Glasgow* at the *Leipzig*. But 'no fall of shot could be seen . . . except an occasional common [shell] bursting short in line with flashes of enemy guns', wrote the *Glasgow*'s gunnery officer. 'The impossibility of observing the fall of shot and the indistinctness of the [target] reduced the chance of hitting

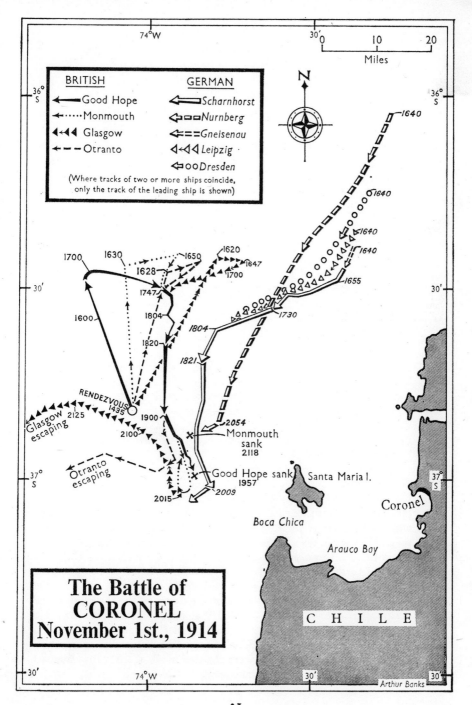

The Battle of
CORONEL
November 1st., 1914

to a minimum.' The *Monmouth*'s fire was at first very rapid though largely wasted since the *Gneisenau* was beyond the range of her 6-inch guns; but after receiving several hits, it became very ragged. The German ships had their own difficulties: according to one of their officers 'the waves rose high in the strong wind. The ships tossed hither and thither. Water foamed up over the small cruisers' forecastles, and then flowed streaming over the upper decks. The guns' crews and ammunition carriers found it difficult to keep their feet'; though von Spee recorded: 'I am of opinion that [the British] suffered more from the heavy seas than we did.' And such was the high standard of training of the German guns' crews and the advantage which the light gave them, that the *Scharnhorst* and *Gneisenau* continued hitting the *Good Hope* and *Monmouth*, whilst the *Glasgow* was straddled by both the *Leipzig* and the *Dresden*.

Within 10 minutes of the Germans first opening fire the result was not in doubt, though Cradock continued to close to the effective range of his 6-inch guns until, by 1935, it was down to 5,500 yards. 'Very frequent hits were observed' on board the *Good Hope* and *Monmouth* by the *Scharnhorst*'s spotting officer, Lieutenant Knoop:

> In most cases hits by high explosive shells were immediately followed by outbreaks of fire. . . . Twice I observed what I believed to be an explosion of ammunition. The flames shot up immediately after hits by high explosive shells and were distinguishable from the other fires by their dimensions and outline. Some hits, probably on the decks, sent up showers of sparks over a wide area. When armour was hit thick black clouds with sharp outlines were observed. Hits were so frequent that it was impossible to note them in chronological order. The *Good Hope* received . . . serious hits . . . in the fore part of the ship . . . on the upper bridge . . . on the mast about thirty feet above the deck . . . [and] on the after side of the foretop. . . . [She] was also hit repeatedly amidships, most of these causing fires. . . . The after battery was hit several times and fires broke out. The flames in the interior of the ship could be seen through the port holes. Two shells struck the ship near the after turret. . . . The *Monmouth* was hit on her fore 6-inch turret. The high explosive shell blew off the roof. . . . A terrific explosion of charges must then have blown the whole turret off the forecastle for it disappeared completely. I observed that many shells struck the ship amidships. . . . A huge column of fire, almost as high as the mast and sixty to ninety feet across, suddenly shot up on the starboard side. . . . Between thirty and forty hits were counted in all. . . . At times three or four fires were burning simultaneously.

An officer aboard the *Glasgow* noted that:

> A continuous sheet of flame appeared along the sides [of the *Good Hope* and *Monmouth*] on which the heavy sea seemed to have no effect. Both ships, however, continued to fight some guns and were rewarded with a few hits. . . . The smoke from their funnels was reddened by the dull glare of the fires below. Frequently either ship flashed into a vivid orange as a lyddite shell detonated against her upper works. By 1945, by which time it was quite dark, *Good Hope* and *Monmouth* were obviously in distress. *Monmouth* yawed off to starboard burning furiously and heeling slightly. *Good Hope*, after three quarters of an hour of action, was firing only a few of her guns. The fires onboard were increasing their brilliance. At 1950 there was a terrible explosion onboard between her mainmast and her after funnel; the gust of flames reached a height of over 200 feet, lighting up a cloud of debris that was flung still higher in the air. She lay between the lines a low black hull lighted only by a dull glow. No one onboard the *Glasgow* actually saw her founder but she could not have survived many minutes.

No one saw the *Good Hope* go down with all hands, including Sir Christopher Cradock, around 2000. But Luce could guess her fate; his ship, which had sometimes been engaging the *Leipzig*, at others the German armoured cruisers, scoring at least one 6-inch hit on the *Gneisenau* (as the poor light permitted fitful observation of the enemy), had so far borne a charmed life, in part due to the difficulty experienced by the *Dresden* and the *Leipzig* in fighting their guns in the prevailing bad weather. One of the *Glasgow*'s officers remembers:

> Looking back it is hard to analyse one's feelings under fire. At first the dreary wail of shells passing over and the higher 'whee-hee' of flying fragments had a peculiarly irritating effect, amounting to childish annoyance at anyone daring to do this to us—an arrogance based on pride of race and astonishment at any outrage on it. The interest in the fight concentrated on one's neighbour. How extraordinarily steady and cool they were. Surely this can't be the real thing. A gun number has the rammer splintered in his hand and doubles across to the disengaged battery: ''ere, Nobby, lend us a rub with your rammer.' A shell bursts on the funnel casing just behind a gun. Only one man has a slight cut from a fragment but it adds a power of hate to the gun's crew as they ram their next projectile viciously home. Three splashes short of the ship—lucky they never ricochetted or else we'd have felt it. A glance on either side expecting to see wounded lying about—not a sign of it, merely business as usual. A dull thud just underfoot—that's a shot on the waterline—more power to the coal that stopped it. Always a fringe of splashes surrounds the ship and yet we escape the hits.

One 4·1-inch shell had made a six-feet-square hole on the *Glasgow*'s waterline above her port outer screw, but it had not stopped her fighting. None the less, now that the German ships were free to concentrate on the *Glasgow* and the *Monmouth*, Luce realised it would be tempting fate to continue the action. His guns could do nothing against such powerful adversaries, whilst every time the *Glasgow* fired a salvo the flashes drew the enemy's fire. So he turned to succour the stricken *Monmouth*, at 2015 signalling her by flashing lamp: 'Are you all right?' Brandt replied: 'I want to get stern to sea. I am making water badly forward.' Luce signalled again: 'Can you steer north-west? The enemy are following us astern.'

> There was no answer [wrote one of the *Glasgow*'s officers]. It was obvious that the *Monmouth* could neither fight nor fly. . . . [She was] badly down by the bows, listing to port with the glow of her ignited interior brightening the portholes below her quarterdeck. . . . It was essential that there should be a survivor of the action to turn *Canopus* which was hurrying at her best speed to join us and, if surprised alone, must have shared the fate of the other ships. *Monmouth* was therefore reluctantly left to her fate, and when last seen was bravely facing the oncoming enemy. *Glasgow* increased to full speed and soon left the enemy astern, losing sight of them about 2050.

'It was an awful affair having to leave the *Monmouth* but I don't see what else the skipper could have done', was the verdict of the *Glasgow*'s gunnery officer. For Edwards, in the *Otranto*, had decided on flight half an hour before: when he realised the *Good Hope* was sorely stricken he had turned his ship sharply to starboard and headed her west at her maximum speed; and Luce could not be sure she would escape the enemy in the night. At 2125, when well to the north-west of the scene of the battle, the *Glasgow* saw 'a searchlight flicker below the horizon. Seventy-five flashes of the firing against *Monmouth* were counted then silence.'

Those final terrible salvoes that sealed the *Monmouth*'s fate came from a ship which had taken no previous part in the action. By 2000 von Spee had lost contact with the British force. Whilst he manœuvred the *Scharnhorst* and *Gneisenau* to the south-west in an attempt to gain the advantage of the moonlight which now illuminated the sombre scene, he wirelessed his light cruisers: 'Both British cruisers severely damaged. One light cruiser apparently fairly intact. Chase the enemy and attack

7 *The German light cruiser* Nürnberg; *the* Dresden, Emden *and* Leipzig *were similar ships*

8 *Von Spee's flagship at Coronel and the Falklands, the armoured cruiser* Scharnhorst; *the* Gneisenau *was a sister-ship*

9   *The British armed liner* Otranto, *part of Cradock's force at Coronel*

10   *The light cruiser* Glasgow, *the only British ship in both battles*

11   *The British battleship* Canopus *which exercised such an unfortunate influence on the battle of Coronel and later defended the Falkland Islands against von Spee's force*

with torpedoes.' The *Leipzig* received this order at about 2105 and complied by steaming at 18 knots towards a dull glare just visible to the north-west. Captain Haun supposed it to be the *Good Hope* burning, but by the time he reached the position there was nothing to be seen from the *Leipzig*'s bridge. Some members of his crew, however, busy jettisoning cartridge cases overboard from the main deck and therefore low down near the water, saw a mass of floating debris that must have come from a sunken ship. But they did not report it to the bridge, a failure that had two results; Haun never had a chance to search for survivors and attempt rescue work, and for several days von Spee remained in ignorance of the British flagship's fate.

Shortly after 2100 Haun sighted three cruisers to the north-west. 'Am between three enemy cruisers; am steering south-west' he wirelessed the *Scharnhorst* and *Gneisenau* towards whom he hoped to draw the enemy; but if one of the ships he sighted was the *Monmouth* or the *Glasgow*, the other two were the *Nürnberg* and the *Dresden*. On receipt of von Spee's order to carry out a torpedo attack, the *Dresden* had steered south-west. At 2030 she sighted the *Glasgow* three and a half miles away turning to a north-westerly course, and tried to follow her, but lost contact before she could engage. She then encountered the *Leipzig* and just recognised her in time to avoid putting a torpedo into her in the belief that she was the *Glasgow*. The *Nürnberg* had been 25 miles from the *Scharnhorst* at 1700 when she received von Spee's signal that Cradock's force had been sighted. Closing at high speed, she had the *Scharnhorst* in sight by 1800, but was still too far away when the action was fought to take any part in it. Von Spee's order to attack with torpedoes was not received until 2054 when von Schönberg turned his ship to a WSW course towards the bearing where he had last seen gunfire. According to von Spee's son, Otto, a lieutenant in the *Nürnberg*:

At 2035 the look-out reported a column of smoke on the starboard bow, for which we at once steered. At first it seemed to approach, then the vessel steamed away at full speed, for although we were going twenty-one knots she rapidly disappeared in the darkness. [This was the *Glasgow*.] During the chase we had occasionally observed a cruiser looking something like the *Leipzig*, steering at first a parallel course to us about two miles on the starboard beam, but then keeping away. When the other fellow got away from us we turned to the second and found it to be the *Monmouth*, heavily damaged. She had a list of about ten degrees to port. As we came nearer she heeled still more, so that she could no longer use her guns on the side turned towards us. We opened fire at short range. It was terrible to have to fire on poor fellows who were no longer able to defend themselves. But their colours were still flying and when we ceased fire for several minutes they did not haul them down. So we ran up for a fresh attack and caused [the *Monmouth*] to capsize by our gunfire. The ship sank with flying colours, and we were unable to save a single man, firstly, on account of the heavy sea, which made it impossible to lower a boat, but also because fresh columns of smoke were reported which we hoped were the enemy's and for which we at once steered. Eventually we found they were our own big cruisers, also looking for the enemy.

The *Monmouth*'s gallant end is accorded a more worthy account by the German official historian. The *Nürnberg*, having discovered a damaged ship—she was seen to be listing between 10 and 15 degrees to port—closed her on that side. Then, to be sure that she was not German, von Schönberg turned a searchlight on her.

She was recognised to be the *Monmouth* with her flag still flying. Her foremost 6-inch turret was missing . . . her engines were running and her steering gear was apparently undamaged as she manœuvred quickly up to the end. As she did not haul down her flag, the *Nürnberg* opened fire at about 2120 at between 1,000 and 600 yards and fired a torpedo from the port side as she turned away; the torpedo missed. . . . The *Nürnberg* then ceased fire as it was not replied to, and switched off her searchlights. The *Monmouth* still kept her flag flying and turned towards the *Nürnberg*, either to ram or to bring her starboard guns to bear. Captain von Schönberg therefore opened fire again, turning at high speed and passing under the *Monmouth*'s stern. . . . The unprotected parts of the *Monmouth*'s hull and also her deck were torn open by the shells. She heeled over further and further and at 2128 she slowly capsized and went down with her flag still flying. Captain von Schönberg subsequently learned that two officers who had been standing on deck heard the *Monmouth*'s officers call the men to the guns; the men were apparently engaged in stopping leaks. There was no chance of carrying out rescue work because columns of smoke were reported to be approaching from two directions (which could be the *Good Hope* and the *Glasgow*). Moreover the ship's boats had been filled with water before the action and could not be launched in the heavy sea. At 2145 the *Nürnberg* reported to the flagship by wireless: 'Have sunk enemy cruiser', and Graf von Spee replied: 'Bravo *Nürnberg*. . . .'

And bravo *Monmouth*! Von Schönberg gave Brandt (or the senior surviving officer at the time) a chance to strike his colours, but in Tudor times British ships established a tradition that they would sink rather than surrender. Admittedly the tradition was not always observed in the eighteenth century, but in the First World War the old indomitable spirit, personified by Sir Richard Grenville, returned: the *Monmouth* was a true descendant of the little *Revenge*.

'Seventy-five flashes . . . and then silence'; it was the end of the Battle of Coronel. By 2215 von Spee decided that the *Glasgow*, the *Otranto* and the *Good Hope* had eluded him. With the first two he had no need to be seriously concerned, and the *Good Hope* he believed to be so heavily damaged that she would have to make for Valparaiso to effect repairs where it was likely he could persuade the Chilean authorities to intern her. But 'against the *Canopus* we can hardly do anything', and from wireless signals which the *Scharnhorst* intercepted, von Spee believed her to be nearing the scene. So he did not risk steaming further to the southward: at 2220 he ordered his light cruisers to form a patrol line on a NNE'ly course, speed 10 knots, with his armoured cruisers following astern until the next morning. Then he gave his ships an opportunity to close his flag and cheer him, responding with the signal: 'By the Grace of God a fine victory. My thanks and good wishes to the crews.' They had 'gone into the fight with enthusiasm', wrote a German authority: 'every man did his duty and contributed to the victory.' Von Spee's satisfaction was fully justified. He had achieved his purpose, command of the sea in the south-east Pacific, at very small cost not least because of the poor quality of the British ammunition; the two shells that hit the *Scharnhorst* had not exploded; the four which struck the *Gneisenau* had caused damage that could soon be repaired, and slightly wounded three men. But he had also expended nearly half his ships' ammunition which could not be replenished. 'The Battle of Coronel will ever be memorable in the annals of [our] Navy', wrote the German official historian. 'On that day von Spee's name was enrolled in the list of German heroes. [He had] materially dimmed the glory of England's mastery of the sea.'

The *Canopus* was not, however, so near as von Spee feared. Since receiving Cradock's signal announcing that he was about to engage the enemy, Grant had left his colliers and pressed his ship hard to reach the scene, but even the $16\frac{1}{2}$ knots which the old ship attained had not brought him much closer than 200 miles of the action. And after Luce had disengaged to the west, the *Glasgow*'s wireless managed to penetrate the barrage of German jamming and warn her of Cradock's defeat. Aboard the *Canopus* were the only members of the *Good Hope*'s crew to survive: Mate Roe and four signal ratings had been landed on Auchile

Island on 29th October to set up an observation post to prevent Cradock's force being surprised while it was coaling in Vallenar Roads.

> My instructions were that if the *Good Hope* had to sail hurriedly I was to make my way by water to the mainland . . . 70–80 miles away. The island was covered with dense vegetation and we had to struggle for four hours to reach the top. When the *Good Hope* left rather quickly early next morning, I was informed that they would let the *Canopus* know where we were, and as she soon came in sight there was no necessity for me to carry out instructions.

Embarked in the *Canopus* and knowing the opinion prevailing in his own ship that she could successfully engage one of von Spee's armoured cruisers but not the pair in company, one can understand his chagrin at Grant's decision, reached at 0200 on the morning of the 2nd, that it was useless for the *Canopus* to continue northward.

> The captain was doubtful what to do; to go on and find the enemy in that sea meant that we should suffer the same fate as the two others and without doing them any damage to speak of [wrote the *Canopus*'s senior engineer, whose judgment is supported by her gunnery officer, who subsequently reported that in the prevailing weather the maximum range of the old battleship's guns was well *inside* that of the German armoured cruisers]. On the other hand it was obviously our duty to cover the retreat of the *Glasgow* which was damaged . . . and the *Otranto*, and also try and save our store ships and colliers. . . . So we turned and steamed full speed back to where our colliers should be. We always steam without lights at night and so do our colliers, and the first thing we knew about them was when we had nearly run into them. We were so glad to find them and gave orders to steam well out into the Pacific and go back to Stanley around the Horn. . . .

The *Glasgow* had suffered four hits from the *Leipzig*'s and *Dresden*'s 4·1-inch shells, in addition to the one already mentioned, but none caused serious damage: and her casualties were negligible. Luce wrote in his report:

> The conduct of the officers, petty officers and men throughout was certainly admirable. Under the trying circumstances of receiving a considerable volume of fire without being able to make an adequate return, perfect coolness and discipline prevailed. . . . The gunlayers behaved exactly as at ordinary battle practice. . . . The efficiency of the engine-room staff speaks for itself when it is stated that a speed of 24 knots . . . was reached a few minutes after the telegraphs were put to full speed ahead, and later a speed of 20 knots was maintained for thirty hours.

The spirit of the officers and men of H.M.S. *Glasgow* is entirely unimpaired by the serious reverse in which they took part, and the unanimous wish of us all is that the ship may be quickly brought to a condition ready to take part in further operations against the same enemy. . . . I cannot close this report without expressing my deepest and sincere regret at the loss sustained by His Majesty's Service in the death of Sir Christopher Cradock and the captains, officers and ships' companies of the *Good Hope* and *Monmouth*, and bearing witness to the determined way in which those ships were fought to the end. Our admiral's gallantry in immediately attacking a superior force, rather than risk the possibility of losing an opportunity by waiting for re-inforcements, though it proved ill-fated, appears to me to be in accordance with the highest traditions of His Majesty's Navy.

Cradock is rightly remembered by a marble memorial unveiled in York Minster in 1916 which bears the inscription:

> *To the Glory of God and in memory of Rear-Admiral Sir Christopher Cradock, Knight Commander of the Royal Victorian Order, Companion of the Most Honourable Order of the Bath, who gallantly upholding the high tradition of the British Navy, led his squadron against an overwhelming force of the enemy off Coronel, on the coast of Chile, and fell gloriously in action on All Saints' Day 1914,*
>
> > *God forbid that I should do this thing,*
> > *To flee away from them;*
> > *If our time be come, let us die manfully*
> > *for our Brethren,*
> > *And let us not stain our Honour.*

There is also a cross in Catherington churchyard, near Portsmouth, which bears the simpler inscription: *In loving memory of Rear-Admiral Sir Christopher Cradock killed in action off Coronel All Saints' Day 1914. His body rests in the Pacific Ocean.*

'Poor Kit, poor Kit Cradock', commented Rear-Admiral Sir Robert Arbuthnot, when he heard the news of the disaster; 'he always hoped he would be killed in battle or break his neck in the hunting field'. And Cradock's old friend, Beatty, wrote to his wife: 'He was a gallant fellow, and I am sure put up a gallant fight, but nowadays no amount of dash and gallantry will counterbalance great superiority unless they are commanded by fools. He has paid the penalty, but doubtless it was better to have fought and lost than not to have fought at all.' The reason why Cradock was beaten is easy to understand; his squadron was all but overwhelmed by a force superior both in the quality of its ships and the efficiency of their crews. And this chapter has explained why, after the *Glasgow* had reported sighting the *Gneisenau* and *Scharnhorst*, Cradock decided to engage von Spee. But whether he was justified in seeking contact, without the support of the *Canopus*, with what he believed to be a single German light cruiser, when he had such limited intelligence of the movements of von Spee's main force, and in the light of the instructions that he had received from the Admiralty, is a much more difficult question—and, after a lapse of nearly 50 years, perhaps a more interesting one to which to attempt an answer.

2

'Armageddon'

'Germany must have a battlefleet so strong that even for the strongest sea power a war against it would involve such dangers as to imperil its position in the world. For this purpose it is not absolutely necessary that the German battlefleet should be as strong as that of the greatest naval power; for such a power will not, as a rule, be in a position to concentrate all its fighting forces against us. But even if it should succeed in meeting us with considerable superiority of strength, the defeat of a strong German fleet would so substantially weaken the enemy that, in spite of the victory he might obtain, his own position in the world would be no longer secured by an adequate fleet.'

From the German Navy Act of 1900

'KIT CRADOCK has gone at Coronel. . . . His death and the loss of the ships and the gallant lives in them can be laid to the door of the incompetency of the Admiralty. They have as much idea of strategy as the Board School boy, and have broken over and over again the first principles.' So Beatty wrote to his wife immediately after receiving news of the disaster on board the *Lion*. He was not alone in condemning the Admiralty for a result which, in the words of the German official historian, 'dealt the most severe blow that British prestige had suffered for over a century. The myth of its invincibility had been ruthlessly destroyed.' The First Lord, Mr Winston Churchill, answered this indictment:

I cannot accept for the Admiralty any share in the responsibility. . . . The first rule of war is to concentrate superior strength for decisive action and to avoid division of forces or engaging in detail. The admiral [Cradock] showed by his telegrams that he clearly appreciated this. The Admiralty orders explicitly approved his assertion of these elementary principles.

43

Was Beatty right to condemn the Admiralty, or was Churchill justified in pleading 'not guilty'? The historian who attempts a just judgment must examine British and German plans for a naval war, the consequent deployment of the two fleets prior to August, 1914, more especially overseas, and the movements of the relevant British and German units after the outbreak of war and the reasons that prompted them, especially of Cradock's force in the light of the telegrams that passed between him and the Admiralty prior to his death. For, in the words of Admiral of the Fleet Lord Wester Wemyss, spoken in 1919,

> there is but one field of naval operations extending over all the world, namely, the sea. . . . Thus it is impossible for a naval commander-in-chief afloat to be the centre whence the strategical direction of naval war radiates. . . . The Board of Admiralty, located in London, is necessarily the centre whence radiate the executive orders as regards operations and movements of ships; and it exercises, as far as the Navy is concerned, many of the functions of the military commander-in-chief in the field. . . .

The nation which Bismarck united accepted Moltke's contention that Germany could never claim to command the sea: in 1872 Germany had only five ironclads, Britain 50. But William II, who ascended the throne in 1890, had greater ambitions; he initiated an aggressive foreign policy: 'Our future lies on the water,' he urged; 'the trident must be in our hands.' Admiral von Tirpitz, whose anglophobia was as near a mania as the All Highest's arrogance, realised this for him: appointed Secretary of State for the Navy in 1897, he immediately launched a campaign which persuaded the Reichstag to pass a Navy Act in 1900 which would not only give Germany a modern balanced fleet but which included in its explanatory memorandum the challenge printed at the head of this chapter. 'The strongest sea power' could only mean Britain: Germany intended to have a fleet which could be so deployed as to be a major threat to it. Britain maintained a significant part of her fleet overseas to protect her immense world-wide interests. If Germany concentrated hers in home waters, it could be strong enough seriously to weaken, if not defeat, such of Britain's Navy as could be deployed against it.

Nevertheless, Germany could not concentrate her *whole* Fleet in the North Sea and Baltic. During the next decade, in which successive Acts built up the German Navy until it became a serious menace to Britain,

> the weighty reasons in favour of the German Empire being represented in foreign waters by her Fleet, and the consequent stationing of modern

cruisers abroad in peace time . . . [which] on the outbreak of war will be unable to rejoin the Home Fleet . . . suggested that these might be used for cruiser warfare. . . . In the narrow sense cruiser warfare is identical with war against commerce; a war against enemy merchant vessels and against contraband carried by neutral vessels. In the wider sense [concluded the German official naval historian] it may include raids on the enemy's coasts, the bombardment of military establishments, the destruction of cables and wireless stations. . . .

The British Empire was particularly vulnerable to this type of warfare, for which Germany made the necessary preparations with typical thoroughness. The few German overseas bases and the impossibility of defending them for long, meant that her cruisers would have to be replenished with coal and other supplies from merchant ships in lonely anchorages. These cruisers would be augmented by arming liners in ports overseas, or at sea from German warships that carried spare guns and ammunition for the purpose. And to enable both types of vessel to attack British trade, and to avoid British warships sent to hunt them down, required an intelligence organisation with tentacles in every neutral country. The German Admiralty also realised that, once war broke out, they would have great difficulty in communicating with their ships overseas: their flag officers and captains would have to operate on their own initiative, rather than under the close control which the British Admiralty intended to exercise over its forces.

When war did come, Germany had eight cruisers overseas, apart from the Mediterranean. Five of them, the already mentioned *Gneisenau*, *Scharnhorst*, *Leipzig* and *Nürnberg*, together with the *Emden*, commanded by Captain Karl von Müller, which was a sister ship of the *Dresden*, formed the East Asiatic Squadron, based on the treaty port of Tsingtau. Of the other three, the *Königsberg* was stationed in East African waters, whilst the *Dresden* was on the western side of the Atlantic whither the *Karlsrühe* had recently been sent to relieve her. For all these ships their war orders stated:

> In the event of a war against Great Britain, or a coalition including Great Britain, ships abroad are to carry on cruiser warfare unless otherwise ordered. Those vessels which are not suitable for cruiser warfare are to fit out as auxiliary cruisers. The areas of operations are the Atlantic, the Indian Ocean, the Pacific. . . . Our ships abroad cannot count in wartime either on reinforcements or large quantities of supplies. . . . The aim of cruiser warfare is to damage enemy trade; this must be effected by engaging equal or inferior enemy forces, if necessary. . . .

The conduct of the naval war in home waters must be assisted by hold-ing as many of the enemy's forces as possible in foreign waters.

Guiding principles for operations in the three areas were then given, those for the Pacific being:

The chief aim of all operations is to damage British trade. Operations, apart from the relative strength and distribution of the belligerent forces, will depend mainly on the possibility of obtaining regular coal supplies. This will also determine the selection of the area of operations: the prompt departure of a ship to this area will oblige the enemy to search for her and consequently to dissipate her forces, thus affording oppor-tunities to achieve tactical success against portions of the enemy's forces. By molesting the main trade routes we may succeed in suspend-ing British traffic in the Far East for a time. The best means of affording relief to Tsingtau is for ships of the Cruiser Squadron to retain their freedom of movement as long as possible. If circumstances are specially favourable for the Cruiser Squadron on the outbreak of war, they may be able to attack enemy forces at once and cripple British trade by winning the supremacy of the seas in the Far East.

The optimism of the last sentence contrasts with the earlier pessimistic suggestion that 'we *may* succeed in suspending British traffic *for a time*'. The reference to Tsingtau shows that Germany had learned the lesson of Port Arthur; to allow the East Asiatic Squadron to be blockaded in port would serve no useful purpose. The Kaiser, as Supreme War Lord, issued more general instructions:

The peace time sailing orders for ships [abroad] become invalid from the moment that an officer in command has an assurance that a war has broken out in which the German Empire is taking part. From that moment he must make his own decisions in the sense of these orders. . . . Above all things, the officer must bear in mind that his chief duty is to damage the enemy as severely as possible. . . . Much more will depend on an officer, when he is in command of a ship operating independently in foreign waters, than is usually the case. The constant strain will exhaust the energy of his crew; the heavy responsibility of the officer in command will be increased by the isolated position of his ship; rumours of all kinds and the advice of apparently well-meaning persons will sometimes make the situation appear hopeless. But he must never show one moment of weakness; he must constantly bear in mind that the efficiency of the crew and their capacity to endure privations and dangers depend chiefly on his personality, his energy and in the manner in which he does his duty. The more difficult and desperate the position,

the more strictly the officer must adhere to the laws of military honour.
. . . If an officer in command succeeds in winning for his ship an honour-
able place in the history of the German Fleet, I assure him of my
Imperial favour. . . .

Before considering, to quote Churchill, 'the magnitude of the task
imposed on Vice-Admiral Graf von Spee at the outbreak of war [by
these orders and instructions, when] he was practically cut off with
nothing but his own resources to depend on, and he had to decide
which of his numerous enemies he should first engage, and which
ocean he should choose as the theatre of his first operation', Britain's
naval war plans and dispositions must be reviewed. When King
Edward VII's coronation ushered in the Indian summer of Britain's
power, there was one man, above all, who understood the challenge
which heads this chapter. 'The new German Navy has come into
existence; it is a navy of the most efficient type and is so fortunately
constituted that it is able to concentrate almost the whole of its fleet
including all its battleships at its home ports', wrote 'Jacky' Fisher in
a paper submitted to the Cabinet immediately he took office as First
Sea Lord in October, 1904, which is best known for begetting H.M.S.
Dreadnought. But it contained another recommendation as important:

> The principles on which the present peace distribution of His Majesty's
> ships and the arrangement of their stations are based, date from a
> period when the electric telegraph did not exist and when the wind
> was the motive power, and it is a wonderful testimony to the strategical
> and political soundness of those principles that they have stood the
> test of time and met all the needs of the Service up to the present
> moment. In the opinion of the Board of Admiralty, however, the new
> conditions . . . have necessitated a review and readjustment of this
> distribution and arrangement of stations.

For a master of the pungent word, the moderation of the last sentence is
surprising, for this 'review and readjustment' was nothing short of
revolutionary. And with his unique drive, Fisher not only achieved it
by the time he left the Admiralty in 1910, but had persuaded the Navy
and the nation to appreciate that it was the one answer to 'the only
thing in the world that England has to fear . . . Germany, and none
else'. He concentrated almost the whole of Britain's capital ship
strength in home waters. Russia's defeat in the Russo-Japanese war and
the Anglo-Japanese Treaty facilitated the withdrawal of the five battleships that had been based on Hong Kong, and the *Entente* allowed him

to remove all except three battle-cruisers from the Mediterranean: by 1914 there remained abroad only the *Triumph* and *Swiftsure*, two hybrid vessels originally built for Chile armed with nothing heavier than 10-inch guns, and the 12-inch-gunned battle-cruiser *Australia*. Fisher supported the British battlefleet, which at the Spithead Review in July, 1914, numbered 59 battleships and battle-cruisers, with squadrons and flotillas of the most modern cruisers and destroyers, all of which went to Scapa Flow and Portland at the beginning of August, 1914, to contain the enemy's main fleet by blockade, until such time as it might be brought to action, thereby ensuring world-wide command of the sea. Secondly, except for a few special cases such as the Yangtse river, he scrapped most of the third-class cruisers, sloops and gunboats which had for so long been stationed in the waters adjacent to Britain's numerous overseas territories, realising that however well they could 'show the flag', put down piracy and assist in dealing with local disturbances, in war they could neither fight nor run away. Instead, he allocated to each foreign station the minimum number of modern cruisers required for these peace-time duties (observing the speed with which communications now enabled them to be dispatched to any trouble spot) as would also suffice in event of war, bearing in mind the ease or otherwise with which reinforcements could be sent from home on mobilisation. These cruisers' prime duty was the protection of Allied shipping against attack by German cruisers and armed merchant cruisers until such time as they could be hunted down and destroyed—but they had many other tasks: escorting convoys bringing troops from overseas, the capture and destruction of German bases, wireless stations and cables, and support for military operations against German colonies.

In the Pacific and the adjacent Indian Ocean these duties were more onerous than elsewhere; for here was Germany's powerful East Asiatic Squadron; here also was her only defended base, Tsingtau; here troops would have to be carried by ships from India, New Zealand and Australia to Suez en route to the Middle East and France; and here were German colonies such as Samoa to be captured, wireless stations such as Yap to be put out of action, and coal stocks such as at Ponapé to be destroyed. Moreover the area, vast in proportion to other oceans, was so far from the United Kingdom that reinforcements could only be sent after a lapse of weeks.

So the British ships available east of Suez at the beginning of August, 1914, (omitting gunboats and other vessels unfit for ocean warfare) numbered: on the China Station, the battleship *Triumph*, the armoured cruisers *Minotaur* and *Hampshire* and the light cruisers *Newcastle* and *Yarmouth*, commanded by Vice-Admiral Sir Martin Jerram; on the East Indies Station, the battleship *Swiftsure* and the light cruisers *Dartmouth* and *Fox* (the last small and obsolete), commanded by Rear-Admiral Sir Richard Pierse; and in Australian and New Zealand waters (where the Dominion Governments had agreed that in war their ships should come under the Admiralty's operational control), the battle-cruiser *Australia*, the light cruisers *Melbourne* and *Sydney* and the obsolete light cruisers *Encounter* and *Pioneer*, under Rear-Admiral Sir George Patey. These ships, in sharp contrast to the Germans', had a whole chain of supply bases and dockyards to support them—Colombo, Singapore, Hong Kong, Sydney, Auckland and many more. And a total of one battle-cruiser, two battleships, two armoured cruisers and five modern light cruisers might seem adequate to deal with von Spee's two armoured cruisers and three light cruisers. (Germany's allies, Austria and Italy, each had a cruiser in Far East waters but neither was of much fighting value.) In fact, half the British ships had other tasks to occupy them: Peirse had to counter the *Königsberg*; Patey had unexpected duties thrust upon him.

The Admiralty appreciated that 'whatever the German force may do, it will require the whole [of Jerram's] force to deal with it', but they were concerned only with matching such force against von Spee as should be adequate to defeat his squadron if it remain concentrated. The difficulty that would be experienced in locating the German ships before they could be brought to action was another matter.

> It is a fair criticism [wrote Churchill] that we ought to have had more fast cruisers in foreign waters [but] the key note of all the Admiralty dispositions at the outbreak of war was to be as strong as possible in home waters. . . . To this end the foreign stations were cut down to the absolute minimum. We grudged every light cruiser removed from home waters, feeling that the [Grand] Fleet would be tactically incomplete without its sea cavalry. The principle of first things first, and of concentrating in a decisive theatre against the enemy's main power, had governed everything . . . the inconvenience in other parts of the globe had to be faced. It was serious.

Jerram could, however, expect some help: in event of war with Germany, France would be an ally, and her alliance with Russia would bring that nation in; and these two countries had in the Far East the armoured cruiser *Montcalm* and the light cruisers *Dupleix*, *Askold* and *Zhemchug*. Much more important, Japan had a whole fleet including 12 capital ships, 11 armoured cruisers and 12 light cruisers. Unfortunately neither the Admiralty nor Jerram could know whether they would have their co-operation, because the Anglo-Japanese Treaty did not require Japan to come to Britain's support should she be involved in war with another European power.

The likelihood of war between Britain and Germany had been clear for so long before August, 1914, that one would suppose Britain's plans for waging it would have been as thorough as Germany's. The contrary was true. 'As I went away,' wrote the Admiralty's Assistant Director of Operations on 5th August, '[Churchill] stopped me, saying he wished to talk about some matters. He said, "Now we have our war. The next thing is to decide how we are going to carry it on." What a statement! The Duke of Newcastle* himself could not have made a more damning confession of inadequate preparation for war.' As a result the Government and the Admiralty, as soon as war began, issued instructions to authorities abroad to execute operations which they had not previously conceived or which ran counter to their own plans. One such decision, which required the full co-operation of the Australian and New Zealand naval forces, was to invite Australia to send expeditions to take New Guinea, Yap and Nauru, and to New Zealand to capture Samoa.

Jerram's plans suffered similarly. Except for the *Newcastle*, which was visiting Nagasaki, and the *Triumph* in reserve at Hong Kong, his ships were at Wei-hai-wei on 28th July when he received the Admiralty's warning of the possibility of war between the Alliance and the *Entente*. He immediately ordered the *Newcastle* to join him, and the *Triumph* to be commissioned. Then, having ascertained that von Spee in the *Scharnhorst* was at or near Yap, the *Gneisenau* (incorrectly owing to a cipher error) at Singapore, and the *Nürnberg* and *Leipzig* as far away as the coast of Mexico, so that the only modern German ship in Chinese waters was the *Emden* at Tsingtau, he signalled the Admiralty on 30th July:

> *Minotaur*, *Hampshire* . . . leaving Wei-hai-wei 1600 today . . . *Newcastle* joins at sea tomorrow . . . *Yarmouth* should arrive Shanghai 2300 tonight and will remain until outbreak of war (*to act as a communication link*). I am sailing to rendezvous north of Saddle Islands and if hostilities commence I hope to prevent *Gneisenau*, *Scharnhorst* from the south . . . reaching Japan.

* Whig Secretary of State, 1724–54, and Prime Minister, 1754–56 and 1757–62.

This was in accordance with Jerram's war plans dated 12th January, 1914, in which he envisaged that he could best protect British trade in China seas by patrolling a line from the mouth of the Yangtse to the south of Japan. The Admiralty had different ideas but did not express them until a signal that crossed Jerram's which began: 'You should concentrate at Hong Kong . . .'. 'As regards this . . . I must confess that I was reluctant to do so', wrote Jerram, 'as it placed me almost 900 miles from what I conceived to be my correct strategical position. I assumed, however, that Their Lordships had good reason for sending me there, and proceeded accordingly. . . .' He reached Hong Kong on 4th August where the whole of his force was concentrated by the 5th. He was joined by the *Dupleix* on the 8th; but the *Montcalm*'s position was unknown even to the French Government, except that she was somewhere in the south Pacific, due at Samoa (German!) on 7th August.

Churchill's zest for war explains why the Admiralty, many thousands of miles away, upset the plans of the man on the spot in this manner. He was no more content to restrict his activities to those normal to the political head of the Admiralty then, than he was to be restrained from becoming akin to Supreme Commander of the whole of Britain's activities on land, sea and in the air 25 years later. It was not enough that an admiral of the calibre of Prince Louis of Battenberg (later Admiral of the Fleet the Marquis of Milford Haven) should be responsible to him for naval operations: on 28th July he sent the First Sea Lord a memorandum which included this paragraph:

> It would certainly be desirable that the *Triumph* should be quickly mobilised and that she should be ready to close [i.e. join] the China flagship. . . . The position of the German heavy cruisers in China waters makes it clear that this can be done. . . . The China Squadron must be capable of concentrating as soon as the warning telegram is sent and before a main action is necessary. Without the *Triumph* the margin of superiority is small, and any reinforcement from other stations would be slow.

Battenberg minuted this: 'Should concentrate at Hong Kong at once', and signalled Jerram accordingly. This memorandum presaged the part Churchill was to play in the Admiralty's responsibility for the results of both Coronel and Falklands, and it shows his appreciation of the need for any British cruiser force likely to encounter von Spee to have a margin of superiority. On the other hand, it also presaged a failure to realise that a slow battleship did not necessarily provide that superiority.

And it displayed the inadequacy of the Admiralty organisation for ensuring that the First Lord and the First Sea Lord were reminded of all relevant factors when making their decisions: the *Australia*, which had the necessary speed as well as gun power, and was already earmarked to join Jerram in war, could have been sent north before the *Triumph* could be commissioned or von Spee's heavy cruisers appear off the China coast, but this was overlooked. Of more immediate importance, however, was the effect of the Admiralty's intervention on the whole of British naval operations over a much wider area than the China Sea. 'Happily', wrote one of the *Emden*'s officers, 'we had in the First Lord of the Admiralty, Churchill, an involuntary ally.' When Jerram received the war telegram early on the morning of the 5th, his force was not in a position to intercept the German ships that sailed from Tsingtau in accordance with signalled orders from von Spee—the armed liner *Prinz Eitel Friedrich*, several colliers, and the light cruiser *Emden*.

The enemy with which Jerram had to deal also included the German liner *Yorck* which had left Yokohama laden with coal and provisions, and the *Scharnhorst*, which the Navy Office, Melbourne, reported to be in the vicinity of the Solomon Islands, possibly with the *Gneisenau* and *Nürnberg* in company. Moreover, the *Leipzig* was reported to have left Mexican waters. So he wrote:

> It seemed probable that the German admiral was:
>
> (*a*) Chasing, or searching for, the *Montcalm*.
>
> (*b*) Proceeding to some rendezvous to coal from colliers which had left Newcastle, N.S.W. on 1st and 2nd August.
>
> (*c*) Proceeding to the South American trade routes. . . .
>
> I regarded it as likely that the German admiral intended to concentrate his forces in the South Seas but . . . I did not feel justified in leaving China Seas to search for him through the southern Pacific Ocean and, moreover, the *Australia*, *Sydney*, *Encounter* and three destroyers were comparatively close to him. I thought it worth while, however, to try to cut off *Emden*, *Yorck* and the four colliers. . . . It seemed likely that they might be bound for Yap . . . and I found that by steaming at 15 knots I could reach Yap before *Emden* and the colliers. *Minotaur*, *Hampshire* and *Newcastle* were the only ships whose coal endurance gave sufficient margin for the purpose, and I decided to take them first to Yap . . . and then to go north to join the remainder of the squadron engaged in watching Tsingtau with a view to preventing the egress of the . . . merchant cruisers believed to be fitting out there.

Jerram's first operation destroyed the wireless station on Yap by bombardment on 12th August, and sank one German collier. His heavy cruisers were not, however, destined to join the *Yarmouth* and *Dupleix* off Tsingtau, for on 11th August the Admiralty intervened again:

> Practically certain Japan declares war against Germany on 12th August. Communicate by wireless with Japanese Commander-in-Chief and concert measures. Send forthwith one light cruiser to close *Rainbow* at Vancouver, coaling at Honolulu. You may now leave whole protection of British trade north of Hong Kong to Japanese, concentrating your attention in concert with Australian Squadron on destroying German cruisers.

Jerram promptly detached the *Newcastle* to the west coast of North America and took the *Minotaur* and *Hampshire* back to Hong Kong to coal, where he arrived on 17th August. And there, for lack of confirmation of Japan's intentions, he signalled the Admiralty:

> Probably *Scharnhorst, Gneisenau, Emden* and *Nürnberg* are now together, but their position is still unknown, though Marshall Islands seem likely. I am watching Tsingtau and arranging to protect trade routes between Japan, Shanghai, Hong Kong, Singapore with all available ships. . . . Possible objective of German squadron may be Dutch East Indies, but more likely Pacific coast of America: in the latter case . . . I suggest for consideration whether it may be possible to spare any cruisers from home waters to meet this danger. Is it still probable Japan will declare war against Germany? . . .

If Japan's hesitation prevented Jerram from initiating further positive action against von Spee, what of Patey, with whom he had been instructed to act in concert, which was by no means easy to arrange over 3,000 miles of intermittent wireless communication between the two flagships? The sudden departure of German colliers from Newcastle, N.S.W. on 4th August, together with intercepted German wireless traffic, initially suggested that the *Scharnhorst* and *Gneisenau* were near New Guinea. So Patey cancelled his original intention to send the *Australia* to Hong Kong and concentrated his squadron near Port Moresby. He then reconnoitred the Bismarck Archipelago and reported on the 13th that the enemy had probably retired to the north or east to coal, sharing Jerram's view that von Spee was most likely to proceed to the South American coast, calling at Samoa or Tahiti on the way. But he was not free to proceed in pursuit: he suddenly learned for the first time that a New Zealand expedition had been sailed to capture Samoa; and since the *Scharnhorst* and *Gneisenau* might well be in that area, he had to detail the *Australia* and *Melbourne* to reinforce its escort, though the French added the *Montcalm* as soon as they located her safe and sound at Suva. To make matters more difficult for Patey, he next heard, also for the first time, that an Australian expedition was already on its way to New Guinea which also needed escorting. But he could only provide the *Sydney* and *Encounter* until the *Australia* should be free from the Samoan expedition, which he appreciated was in greater danger from attack. The principle laid down by the Committee of Imperial Defence that all overseas operations were to make the protection of sea communications their primary aim had given way before the endeavour to occupy the largest possible extent of Germany's territory overseas. The Committee was not to be blamed for this: 'There was one question which we never did succeed in getting tackled before the war, namely the working out of plans for the capture of the German colonies', wrote their secretary, Captain Hankey (now Lord Hankey) '[The War Office] was strongly opposed to any investigation of the kind on the grounds that any [such] plans . . . were certain to lead to dispersion of force in "side-shows".' The War Office might be thinking of a war in France, but it evinced more foresight than the wisdom shown by the Government and the Admiralty once hostilities had begun. One must not however be too critical of the decision to authorise these expeditions against small isolated German colonies, whose capture could have been undertaken without prejudice or difficulty at any time convenient to Patey (though it is less easy to forgive their omission to keep him informed of their intentions). This was the first major war in which cables and wireless provided Whitehall with the means of intervening directly in the conduct of overseas operations. Although a cable linking London with the Crimea had made this possible as far back as 1866, there had been no parallel development in government machinery for the conduct of war, which remained almost as simple as it had been in Napoleonic times when communications were as slow as the horse and the sailing vessel. To quote Hankey again: 'Although the C.I.D. provided machinery for the exercising of the Supreme Command in peace, nothing had been thought out on the Supreme Command in war. [Not until] after the war [was] a remedy provided by the formation [in 1924] of the Chiefs of Staff Sub-Committee.' In his book *Walpole*, John Morley wrote: 'The flexibility of the Cabinet system allows the Prime Minister in an emergency to take upon himself a power not inferior to that of a dictator, provided always that the House of Commons will stand by him.' But Asquith was not the man to exercise this power; he could not appreciate that a Cabinet of 21 members was no better than a debating society when it came to the conduct of a major war. It was not equipped to take vital decisions, based on proper consideration of all aspects of the problem, including the necessary professional advice, least of all when, as inevitably happened, decisions were required at very short notice. And this deficiency was accentuated when authorities abroad regarded instructions from London as next to sacrosanct instead of subjecting them to a healthy review on the grounds that Whitehall, half the world away, could not always be wiser than the man on the spot. Jerram's quiescent attitude towards the Admiralty's instructions to concentrate at Hong Kong is an example of this.

British and Allied warships in the Far East were thus deployed when, on 23rd August, Japan declared war. This changed the situation considerably. Though Jerram was required to allocate some of his ships to assist the Japanese investment of Tsingtau, this port was no longer of value to Germany, and its fall could be taken as certain. (It surrendered on 7th November.) More important, the Japanese Fleet became available for operations against von Spee, which ruled out the possibility that he would return to the north-west Pacific and released Jerram's cruisers for operations in southern waters.

The actual movements of the German East Asiatic Squadron immediately before, and in the days following, the outbreak of war, must now be traced in contradistinction to the limited intelligence about them available to Jerram and Patey. The armoured cruisers *Scharnhorst* and *Gneisenau* had left Tsingtau at the end of June for a three months' cruise in the south-west Pacific. They were to be joined at Samoa in August by the light cruiser *Nürnberg* from the west coast of Mexico whither the *Leipzig* had gone to relieve her, which left von Müller, captain of the *Emden*, as senior officer in Chinese waters. Von Spee, his flag in the *Scharnhorst*, was thus at Truk on 7th July when Berlin signalled that the 'political situation is not entirely satisfactory'. The warning could hardly have been in vaguer terms; to its recipient, 10,000 miles away from the Wilhelmstrasse, it conveyed no more than the possibility of war with one or more unnamed European Powers. Whether these would include Britain, the only one with a force in Far Eastern waters comparable with the German East Asiatic Squadron, he had no means of determining. But it seemed wise to await further developments at Ponapé, where he arrived a week later, and to order the *Emden* to postpone a projected cruise up the Yangtse in which she might be too easily blockaded. Further warning signals reached von Spee during the next three weeks, but none of them did much to clarify the situation until, on the 27th, he was told: 'Strained relations between Dual Alliance and Triple *Entente* are possible. The Samoan cruise will probably have to be abandoned. *Nürnberg* has been ordered to proceed to Tsingtau. Everything else is left to you.' Von Spee responded immediately to the last sentence; aware that a war with Britain was likely to bring in Japan, a country with a whole fleet available to invest Tsingtau, it seemed wholly wrong to send the *Nürnberg* there. So he signalled Berlin an urgent request to divert her to join him at Ponapé.

'Imminent danger of war with Great Britain, France and Russia', was the next news to reach von Spee, on 1st August. Four days later, whilst still at Ponapé, he heard that Britain had begun hostilities in a signal that also contained two portentous sentences: 'Chile is a friendly neutral', and 'Japan will remain neutral'. The latter was the most important: von Spee's war plans, which he had frequently discussed with Berlin in the past two years and finally issued in the spring of 1914, embodied the following principles. Whilst Britain's overall command of the sea would stop German maritime trade in most areas, this could be mitigated in the Pacific by keeping his squadron together, since it would force the enemy to concentrate his own ships. In so large an ocean this might reduce the chances of German merchant ships being located and captured and allow trade to continue, albeit on a reduced scale. It would also minimise the danger of von Spee's squadron being located except in favourable circumstances. To carry out this policy the German cruisers must not allow themselves to be shut in Tsingtau. If Japan remained neutral, they must prevent it being blockaded and permit its continued use as a coaling base by attacking enemy trade in Chinese and Japanese waters, and down as far as the Malacca Straits; their protection would fully occupy the British China Squadron. If, on the other hand, Japan entered the war, Tsingtau would have to be abandoned; the East Asiatic Squadron would then transfer its operations to another area, against which eventuality arrangements had been made for the requisite supply ships.

In line with these principles, von Spee had issued the following orders to Captain Müller shortly before leaving Tsingtau:

In the event of strained relations . . . the [heavy] cruisers in the South Seas will endeavour to concentrate and proceed in the direction of Tsingtau, in order to safeguard coal supplies for future operations. The coal supplies for their return must be assured. The *Emden* is to protect the colliers leaving Tsingtau, but must not allow herself to be blockaded there. The colliers are to proceed to Pagan Island. The *Emden* will then endeavour to join the main body. . . .

Accordingly, after the *Nürnberg* had arrived at Ponapé on 5th August, von Spee, with the knowledge that the British China Squadron was at Hong Kong, and the powerful *Australia* to the south of him, sailed his three cruisers for Pagan, in the Mariana Islands, 1,000 miles to the north, where he arrived on the 11th. And here on the 12th he was joined by the *Emden*, the *Prinz Eitel Friedrich*, the *Yorck* and four of the supply vessels from Tsingtau that had eluded Jerram's ships. There had been four more, but one had been sunk by the *Minotaur*, as already noted, whilst one had been captured by the *Triumph* and two by the *Dupleix*. This 50 per cent loss was proof of the difficulties von Spee expected in keeping his squadron supplied; but German naval agents in Manila, Shanghai, and Tokyo were already busy sailing more colliers to rendezvous in the Pacific which the German admiral had specified in his war orders.

Having coaled his force at Pagan, von Spee did not, however, pursue his intention to proceed against British trade in East Asiatic waters. He learned that Japan might, after all, enter the war against Germany. Berlin's signalled sentence, 'Chile is a friendly neutral', was now the more important. 'If the Japanese try to impose conditions, it would be best for the Cruiser Squadron to proceed to the west coast of America, because coal would be most easily obtainable there. It would be much too risky to remain in the Indian Ocean', his war diary records. A second consideration was the news that Jerram had left Hong Kong for the southward, followed by the destruction of the German wireless station at Yap.

> [My] force will not be able to hold its own against a superior enemy and must disappear for a time in order to escape destruction and to remain as a 'fleet in being' in order to cause anxiety to the enemy, and appear elsewhere when opportunity occurs to do good service. If we proceed to the Indian Ocean we should be faced by the impossibility of obtaining fuel . . . we have no coaling bases in the Indian Ocean and no agents whom we can get in touch with. If we proceed towards the American coast we shall have both at our disposal. . . .

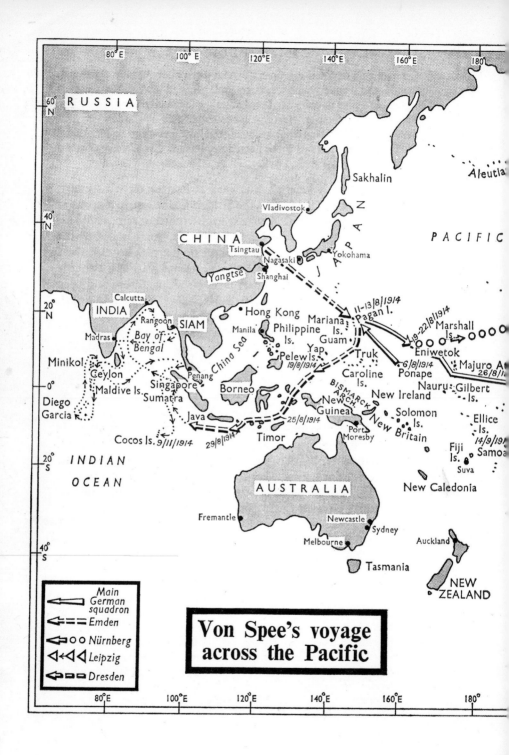

Von Spee's voyage across the Pacific

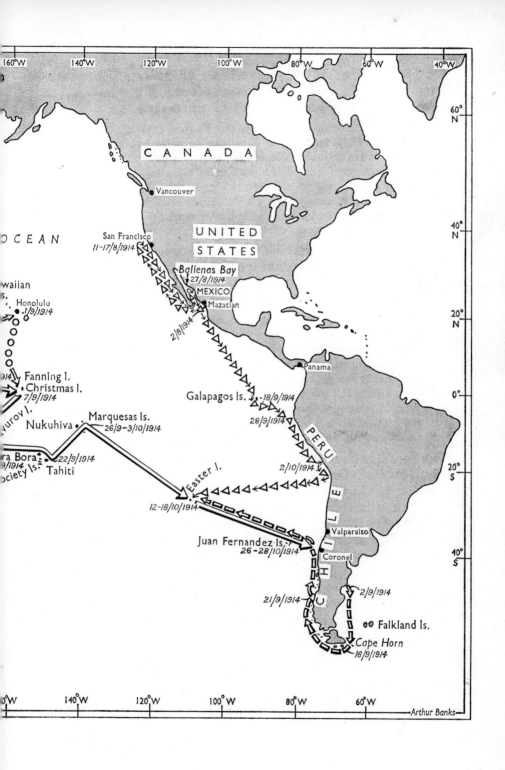

CANADA

Vancouver

UNITED
STATES

OCEAN

waiian

Honolulu
1/9/1914

San Francisco
11-17/8/1914

Ballenas Bay
27/8/1914

MEXICO

Mazatlan

2/8/1914

Fanning I.
Christmas I.
7/9/1914

urov I.

Galapagos Is.
·18/9/1914

28/9/1914

Panama

Marquesas Is.
26/9–3/10/1914

Nukuhiva

PERU

ra Bora
9/1914
ociety Is.

22/9/1914
Tahiti

Easter I.

2/10/1914

12-18/10/1914

CHILE

Juan Fernandez Is.
26–28/10/1914

Valparaiso

Coronel

21/9/1914

2/9/1914

Falkland Is.

Cape Horn
16/9/1914

Arthur Banks

On the morning of 13th August, von Spee called his captains to a conference on board the *Scharnhorst*: Schultz, Maerker of the *Gneisenau*, von Schönberg of the *Nürnberg* and von Müller were there.

> The Commander-in-Chief [wrote the *Emden*'s captain] developed his views on the situation and the most practical employment of the squadron. He drew attention to the threatening attitude of Japan and to the advantage of maintaining the Cruiser Squadron together and concealing its whereabouts and aims as long as possible, thereby holding a large number of enemy ships. He also laid emphasis on the difficulties of obtaining coal. . . . He had decided, after careful consideration, to take the squadron first to the west coast of America.

Thus was the decision taken that was to lead to a German victory off Coronel, a decision whose strong possibility had been realised by both Jerram and Patey. But something else was said at this conference that was to have dramatic consequences in another part of the world.

> When we commanding officers were asked for an expression of opinion, I [von Müller] said I was afraid that the Cruiser Squadron would be able to do practically nothing during a long cruise in the Pacific, and that I thought it questionable whether so much value should be attached to the 'fleet in being' theory. If coaling the whole squadron in East Asian, Australian and Indian waters presented too great difficulties, I asked whether we might consider the dispatch of at least one light cruiser to the Indian Ocean. The Commander-in-Chief replied that . . . he would consider the advisability of sending the *Emden* there. . . .

Von Spee did not take long to make up his mind. 'A single light cruiser which consumes far less coal and can, if necessary, coal from captured steamships, will be able to maintain herself longer than the whole squadron in the Indian Ocean; and as there are great prizes to be won there, it seems advisable to dispatch our fastest light cruiser, the *Emden*, with our best collier. . . .' That evening, 13th August, the German East Asiatic Squadron left Pagan with its supply ships; and early on the 14th the *Emden*, with the collier *Markomannia* in company, was detached to the Indian Ocean. As he parted company von Müller signalled: 'I thank your Excellency for the confidence placed in me. I wish the Cruiser Squadron a successful cruise.' He was soon to do much to justify von Spee's confidence in him.

The squadron had a rough passage eastwards at the slow speed of its supply ships, 7–10 knots, but its morale was high. 'We have been cruising since 26th June', wrote a German seaman in a letter home. 'In Ponapé we mobilised our ships, *Scharnhorst*, *Gneisenau*, and *Nürnberg*.

On 5th August we learned that war had been declared. On the 6th we left Ponapé. In the afternoon Graf von Spee made a fitting speech to our crew which ended in three hearty cheers for the Emperor and Empire. The feeling aboard was excellent. On 19th August we reached the Marshall Islands.' Here, in the spacious Eniwetok Atoll lagoon, von Spee's force coaled again, secure in the knowledge from intercepted wireless traffic that the nearest enemy force, the Australian Squadron, was far to the westward.

> After three days coaling we put to sea again. Owing to being at war, we cease coaling at dark and are continuously under steam ready to proceed. Our repairs have to be carried out during watchkeeping. We have many 'clear ship for action' exercises. You may believe all this tires us. But one gets used to anything. The main point is that we win the war and return home safe and sound.

From Eniwetok von Spee sent the *Prinz Eitel Friedrich* and *Cormoran* to raid trade routes in Australian waters. And when the squadron sailed on 22nd August he detached the *Nürnberg* to Honolulu with mails and signals to be sent by cable to Berlin which included his future intentions, notably: 'I shall proceed to Chile . . . arriving at Juan Fernandez on 15th October', and the coal he required to be sent there from San Francisco and Valparaiso. Since the enemy would know that the *Nürnberg* had recently left Mexican waters, her appearance at the U.S. port of Honolulu would not compromise the movements of von Spee's heavy cruisers. These reached Majuro Atoll, another spacious lagoon at the south-eastern end of the Marshall Islands, where, once again, they coaled. And there, on the 26th, the admiral received news of Japan's declaration of war, which confirmed the soundness of his decision to proceed towards South America.

In view of what has been said about Whitehall's intervention in the operations of British forces overseas, it is of interest to note the wisdom of Berlin's different attitude. On 18th August the German Naval Staff made this appreciation:

> The Cruiser Squadron intended, in the event of war with Great Britain, to proceed from the South Seas to Tsingtau. It may be assumed that it is now in East Asiatic waters. The news of Japan's impending entry into the war makes its position hopeless. It is impossible to judge from here whether the squadron will be able to choose against which enemy it will deal its dying blows. If the choice does not rest with it, it is useless to issue any orders. If the choice does still rest with it, an attack on Japanese forces or on their communications would seem advisable. It

would undoubtedly be the best plan if there were any chance of saving Tsingtau, but as that appears to be out of the question, it is useless to issue orders in this case also. Further, we are ignorant of the Commander-in-Chief's dispositions regarding coal supplies and, judging from his oft repeated utterances, it may be taken for granted that he will attempt to bring the enemy to action. Whether he engages the British or the Japanese must depend on their relative situations, and any interference on our part might be disastrous. The Commander-in-Chief must have complete liberty of action as hitherto. If he succeeds in beating the British before the Japanese have time to come in we should regard it as a great achievement. Even if he were able, contrary to all probability, to transfer his activities to another ocean, it would be wrong for us to interfere with his freedom of action. Should he succeed in reaching the Atlantic Ocean he might damage the British far more seriously than in the Far East and might also contrive to maintain his squadron there for a longer period, thanks to former preparations. In view of the above it is better to send no instructions to the Commander-in-Chief.

So no instructions were sent, least of all after Berlin received, via Honolulu, the news of von Spee's movements and intentions. There was only a single signal from the Kaiser which von Spee never received: 'God be with you in the impending stern struggle. My thoughts accompany you.'

Observing the several errors in their appreciation, it is easy to agree with Berlin that 'any interference on our part might be disastrous'. Moreover, von Spee had more than justified their trust in him. Indeed, one must agree with the German official historian that his 'was a brilliant achievement on the part of a commander-in-chief on whom all responsibility rested for, being cut off from home, he was entirely dependent on his own resources and in drawing up his plans he had to consider what the situation might be in almost every part of the world'.

> He had [wrote Churchill] no lack of objectives. He had only to hide and to strike. The vastness of the Pacific and its multitude of islands offered him their shelter and, once he had vanished, who should say where he would reappear. On the other hand, there were considerable checks on his action and a limit, certain though indefinite, to the life of his squadron. . . . He was a cut flower in a vase, fair to see yet bound to die. [But so long as he lived] all our enterprises lay simultaneously under the shadow of a serious potential danger. . . . Von Spee and his squadron could turn up almost anywhere. On the other hand we could not possibly be strong enough every day everywhere to meet him.

'Von Spee . . . could turn up almost anywhere'—but it was to be more than three weeks before he did. Meantime, following Japan's declaration of war, a whole series of movements and concentrations of British and Allied warships were ordered to minimise the threat the German squadron presented, which were made doubly difficult by the unexpected appearance of the *Emden* in another ocean. Before, however, considering these developments, we may pause to review von Spee's decisions. First, he was surely right not to proceed further north than Pagan with his initial intention to attack British trade in East Asiatic waters. The best Germany could hope for was that Japan would remain neutral; and that hope was so tenuous that offensive operations in waters close to the Japanese islands must antagonise her to the point of war. And once Japan decided on war, the massive strength of her fleet must make it impossible for a small German force, its base rendered untenable by blockade, to achieve anything of value; nor could it survive for long without being located and destroyed. But von Spee's subsequent decisions raise questions which are by no means so easy to answer. Was he right to keep his force concentrated, the *Emden* excepted? And was he right to escape the double claws of the Japanese and British squadrons to the north, and the Australian and New Zealand squadrons to the south, by steaming eastward into the Pacific? His reasons for doing so have been presented; but was his victory at Coronel, and the cessation of British trade on the west coast of South America that followed, sufficient justification? Before Coronel he did little for more than two months except disappear into the vast waters of the Pacific. This occupied Allied ships in protecting various operations against the possibility that they might be attacked; but there was practically no British trade, nor were there other objectives of any importance in that area against which von Spee could carry out cruiser warfare.

Would he then, have done more damage if he had taken his squadron into the Indian Ocean, leaving the *Leipzig* alone in the Pacific? There were many more objectives in the Indian Ocean—important trade routes, troop convoys, ports and cable stations—against which the German ships might have done great damage. And there was the Cape, where the arrival of German warships might have bolstered a Boer rebellion against the Government's intended invasion of German South-West Africa, just as the *Goeben* and *Breslau*'s arrival in the Bosphorus encouraged Turkey to join the Alliance. The difficulties von Spee expected in obtaining coal for his squadron in the Indian Ocean may be a sufficient argument against this course. On the other hand, the greater damage he could have done there might have made this hazard worth accepting. Moreover, though it might have been difficult to coal his ships for so long as they remained concentrated as a squadron, this might not have been true if they had operated independently. And it would have taken the Allies a long time to locate and destroy four German cruisers operating alone, especially when two of them were armoured cruisers requiring ships as strong to combat them, of which the Allies could only spare a limited number outside the North Sea.

To all these points there can be no firm answers. Too many factors, too many imponderables are involved, not the least being the different personalities and capabilities of the captains of the German ships. The fate of the *Königsberg* is evidence against the chances of a lone cruiser achieving much in the Indian Ocean. After sinking one British liner in the first week of the war, and the obsolete cruiser *Pegasus* on 20th September, she was content to seek refuge up the Rufigi river; after which she was no more than a nuisance, in that it took some weeks to locate her there, and much longer to send out from home the monitors needed to destroy her. On the other hand the exploits of the *Emden*, a light cruiser of 3,600 tons armed with nothing heavier than ten 4·1-inch guns, and with a maximum speed of 24 knots, showed the damage that could be caused by a single vessel commanded by a man of outstanding ability.

The 41-year-old Karl von Müller had been born in the same mould as the French privateer captains of the eighteenth century: he combined single-minded audacity with clear-headed skill, courage with chivalry. His exploits are a classic example of cruiser warfare in a sea dominated by superior enemy forces. The shipping he captured, a total of 23 vessels of an estimated value of £2,200,000 in the course of 70 days in the Indian Ocean, is no real measure of his success: the *Emden* did much more than that for the German cause; and not the least of von Müller's triumphs was the way in which, for all this time, he kept his ship supplied with coal in an area which had none of the facilities available to von Spee in the Pacific. But the chief reason for summarising the *Emden*'s career in these pages is the effect which it had on the Allies' plans for dealing with von Spee's squadron.

The *Emden* began her marauding career in the Bay of Bengal: between 10th and 14th September, in the approaches to Calcutta, she sank or captured eight steamers before the Admiralty learned that she was no longer with von Spee in the Pacific. All vessels trading in the Bay of Bengal were immediately held in port and traffic was stopped on the Colombo–Singapore route, thus depriving von Müller of further prey, whilst the hunt for him began. For the genesis of this, it is necessary to go back to the day Japan declared war, 23rd August. Since the intervention of her Fleet ruled out the possibility of von Spee appearing in East Asiatic waters, Jerram made a fresh appreciation:

> I was aware that the whole of the Australian and New Zealand Squadrons and the *Montcalm* were well to the eastward of Australia engaged in escorting expeditions, first to Samoa and then to New Britain . . .; that the best ships of the East Indies Squadron were engaged in escorting troops from India westwards; and that the only British force on the great trade routes between Colombo, Singapore and Australia were the *Fox* and *Expiègle* [sloop] near Colombo, and the *Pioneer* near Fremantle. I have mentioned the possibility of the Germans going to the Dutch East Indies, and bearing in mind the disastrous results to our trade if they did so, the conclusion was irresistible, that a strong force was needed to work from Singapore.

Thus, Jerram, who could not be sure of von Spee's destination, judged he should guard against the German squadron doubling back to strike in an area where the prizes to be had were so valuable. Patey, on the other hand, preoccupied with escorting expeditions that should never have been launched whilst von Spee was at large in the Pacific, still believed the Germans' destination to be South America, calling at Samoa and Tahiti. But when signalling this to Jerram, he added that attacks by German armed merchant cruisers were likely on the trade routes to China and Australia.

The Admiralty appreciated that von Spee might be on his way to South America; telegrams to London from the British consul-generals in Valparaiso and Buenos Aires reporting that German ships, and neutral ones chartered by German agents, were being sailed to Chilean waters and the Straits of Magellan laden with coal and provisions indicated this. So they signalled Jerram:

> How is China Squadron disposed? Destruction of *Scharnhorst* and *Gneisenau* is of first importance. Proceed on this service as soon as possible with *Minotaur*, *Hampshire* and *Dupleix*, keeping in communication with R.A. *Australia* [Patey] who, together with *Montcalm*, is engaged on same service. They are at present searching for them at Samoa. . . .

But it is difficult to know whether to be more astonished at the Admiralty's apparent ignorance of Jerram's dispositions; at the absence of any indication of whither he should 'proceed on this service', or at the delusion that Patey was already searching for von Spee in Samoan waters. Indeed, it is impossible to believe that such a signal could have been drafted by a professional naval staff and dispatched on the authority of the First Sea Lord or the Chief of Staff. It bears the hallmark of an amateur; its phrasing is Churchillian. The consequences in this case may not have been important; but it is a characteristic example of the unsatisfactory way in which the Admiralty functioned in the first months of the war.

One cannot therefore be surprised at Jerram's reaction. Charts and mails found onboard a prize out of Tsingtau indicated (erroneously) that the German squadron might be in the Java Sea, using the Dutch Islands as their base. So he took the *Minotaur* and *Hampshire* down to Singapore, followed by the *Dupleix*, the *Yarmouth* and the Japanese cruisers *Ibuki* and *Chikuma*, leaving the *Triumph* to assist the Japanese with their attack on Tsingtau, and began a systematic search of the East Indies. But this proved so fruitless that, on his return to Singapore a fortnight later, he signalled the Admiralty:

> There is absolutely no news of *Scharnhorst* and *Gneisenau* since 9th August. . . . I consider it possible or even probable they will be heard of on South American coast and that they will attack our trade either off Straits of Magellan or off mouth of River Plate. I consider the only solution is to establish my headquarters [ashore] and send *Minotaur* and *Hampshire* to join C.-in-C. Australia.

Patey could have done with these reinforcements because on 1st September he had been warned of yet another commitment for his ships, to detach the *Sydney* and *Melbourne* to escort the first Australian and New Zealand troop convoy which was to leave for Europe on 22nd September. The importance the Admiralty attached to this convoy was stressed by their reply to Jerram: his decision to transfer his flag ashore was approved, but the *Hampshire* was to proceed to Fremantle to join the convoy's escort which Patey was to augment with the *Australia*. The movements of the *Minotaur*, the Admiralty added, would be settled later. Jerram consequently assumed that they did not share his latest assessment of von Spee's intentions: he arranged for the *Minotaur*, *Ibuki* and *Chikuma* to proceed to New Britain against the possibility of the German East Asiatic Squadron threatening Australian waters whilst

13　*Von Spee's East Asiatic Cruiser Squadron on its way across the Pacific*

14   *The Australian light cruiser* Sydney *which destroyed the* Emden

15   *The German light cruiser* Emden *on North Keeling Island
after her action with H.M.A.S.* Sydney

Patey was at Samoa. These plans were, however, thrown into the melting pot 48 hours after Jerram's return to Singapore by the first news of the *Emden*'s activities. Knowing that there were no other Allied warships in the Bay of Bengal, least of all Pierse's East Indies Squadron, he at once sailed the *Hampshire*, Captain H. W. Grant, the *Yarmouth* and *Chikuma* to search for her.

Something more important happened very soon after this; in circumstances to be related later, the *Scharnhorst* and *Gneisenau* appeared off Apia in Samoa, already occupied by the New Zealand expedition; and by 16th September the Admiralty at last had positive news of von Spee's armoured cruisers. As one result the *Minotaur* and the *Ibuki* were ordered to Fremantle to take the place of the *Hampshire* in the escort of the Australian–New Zealand troop convoy.

Meantime, von Müller had moved from the approaches to Calcutta, to Rangoon, but he found nothing there except a single Norwegian freighter on 18th September. His activities had locked Allied merchant ships in port; moreover, from intercepted chatter between the operators of shore wireless stations, he realised that Grant's force was after him. So he decided to strike against British interests elsewhere: after dark on the 22nd he approached the port of Madras unobserved, and bombarded and set on fire the oil tanks. This incident made a deep impression throughout India and seriously disturbed trade in the area, but though the need to find and destroy such a dangerous marauder was clearly urgent, the task was beyond Jerram's limited resources. And Pierse could not help: his war orders had specified patrols for five focal points on the trade routes, one the little coral island of Minikoi, 400 miles west of Colombo; but, as with Jerram and Patey, his plans had been upset by unexpected orders from home giving precedence to escorting convoys carrying the Indian Army to Egypt and France; he was left with nothing to protect the trade which von Müller made his next objective. Off Minikoi, between 25th and 27th September, the *Emden* took six Allied ships before her presence was reported, and the *Hampshire* and her consorts could pursue her, by which time the lone wolf had sought refuge in the Maldive Islands.

Von Müller was next misled by an old chart to make an abortive visit to the Chagos Archipelago, 600 miles south of the Maldives, before he moved to lonely Diego Garcia to give his ship and her crew a much needed rest. Thence he made a second foray against the Minikoi focal point with results as profitable as before; he sank or captured six Allied merchant ships between 16th and 19th October with the result that the

Allies at last stirred themselves to drastic action to counter his depredations. The Admiralty ordered the light cruiser *Gloucester* from the
Mediterranean, and, following the discovery of the *Königsberg* up the
Rufigi river, released the light cruisers *Dartmouth* and *Weymouth* for the
same service. But these orders were changed after the news of Coronel,
it being supposed that South Africa was one of von Spee's possible
destinations: the orders to the *Dartmouth* were countermanded, the
Minotaur, which with the *Ibuki*, *Melbourne* and *Sydney* had at last left
Australia on 1st November for Colombo with the first big convoy of
Australian and New Zealand troops, was ordered to Simonstown,
whilst, to make up for these withdrawals, the Japanese sent a cruiser
squadron into the Bay of Bengal. But the net thus spread to enmesh von
Müller could not be immediately effective: he was able to steam unde-
tected as far east as the Nicobar Islands and thence to carry out the most
audacious of all his exploits. At dawn on 28th October he entered
Penang Roads and sank the anchored Russian cruiser *Zhemchug* and a
French destroyer.

Von Müller's next decision was, however, to be his last.

> The possibility of Cocos Island being seized by the *Emden* had been
> constantly in my mind [wrote Jerram] and although I could not possibly
> spare a ship to be stationed there permanently, I had instructed the cable
> station as to the precautions to adopt and the necessity of giving
> immediate warning in the event of surprise attack.

So, when early on the morning of the 9th November, a strange warship
was sighted approaching the island, the cable staff immediately gave
the alarm. And this was heard by the *Melbourne*, Captain Silver, senior
officer of the escort for the Australian troop convoy which, all unknown
to von Müller, was then only 55 miles to the north of Cocos on its way
to Colombo. H.M.A.S. *Sydney* was at once ordered to raise steam for full
speed and proceed to Cocos. Two and a half hours later Captain Glossop
opened fire with such effect that at 1120 von Müller beached his wrecked
and burning ship on North Keeling Island and surrendered.

Such was the end of the first ship of von Spee's squadron to be
destroyed. Von Müller merited the Iron Cross, First Class, which the
Kaiser bestowed upon him. To quote the *Nordeutsche Allgemeine
Zeitung*:

> For three full months, under the most difficult conditions, the *Emden*,
> with tenacious courage and exemplary seamanship, has harried the
> enemy and caused them heavy losses. Finally she had to succumb to

the hunt organised for her by British, Russian, French and Japanese warships. [But] the name *Emden* will live in the memory of the German people to all posterity:

whilst the *Daily Telegraph* said:

> It is almost in our heart to regret that the *Emden* has been captured or destroyed. . . . He [von Müller] has been enterprising, cool and daring in making war on our shipping, and has revealed a nice sense of humour. He has, moreover, shown every possible consideration to the crews of his prizes. . . . There is not a survivor who does not speak well of this young German, the officers under him and the crew obedient to his orders. The war on the sea will lose something of its piquancy, its humour and its interest now that the *Emden* has gone.

With the *Königsberg* bottled up in the Rufigi river, and von Spee's squadron known to be in South American waters (for this was a week after Coronel) the sinking of the *Emden* greatly lightened the tasks of Jerram, Patey and Pierse and of all the Allied vessels that had been hunting for her in the Indian Ocean. Maritime trade vital to the war effort could now flow unhindered across it, and transports carrying troops and guns to the Middle East and the Western Front could proceed without interruption. But, remembering the questions posed earlier as to whether von Spee was right to take his main force away from the Indian Ocean, one cannot but wonder at the havoc that might have been caused, and the time and effort which would have been needed to hunt them down, if the *Scharnhorst*, *Gneisenau* and *Nürnberg* had operated there with the same skill and audacity as von Müller's famous ship.

3

Cradock's Odyssey

'Probably *Scharnhorst, Gneisenau* . . . *Nürnberg* are now together. . . . Possible objective of German squadron . . . Pacific
coast of America. . . . Suggest for consideration whether it
may be possible to spare any cruisers from home waters to
meet this danger. . . .'
Commander-in-Chief China to Admiralty, 17th August, 1914

LONG BEFORE 15th September, when von Spee was first definitely
located as far east as Apia, both Jerram and Patey had several times
signalled the Admiralty that South America was the Asiatic Squadron's
most likely destination. Indeed, Jerram sent such a signal within a
fortnight of the outbreak of war which included the suggestion which
heads this page. What steps, then, did the Admiralty take to guard
against an eastward move by von Spee?

British war plans recognised the special importance of protecting
trade in the Atlantic; here was a greater volume of shipping to be
safeguarded than in any other ocean. The threat amounted to two German cruisers in the western Atlantic and one in the Azores, plus a
number of liners which were expected to emerge from American ports
as armed merchant cruisers. Since a trained fleet in home waters
superior to the German High Seas Fleet, which should also be able to
prevent any additional German warships breaking out into the Atlantic,
was given first priority, the number of cruisers allocated for overseas
duty in peace was small. In the Atlantic there should have been no
more than the *Glasgow* in South American waters, her sister, the *Bristol*,
in Cradock's North America and West Indies command, and three
vessels of small fighting value at Simonstown to deal with Germany's
African colonies. Civil war in Mexico, and the consequent need to
protect British interests there had, however, enforced one important

change: Cradock had been given the Fourth Cruiser Squadron, the *Suffolk* (flag), *Berwick*, *Essex* and *Lancaster*, all sister-ships of the *Monmouth*; whilst, for the same reason, the French had sent the cruisers *Descartes* and *Condé*.

But even with these additions, the Allied navies in the Atlantic could neither provide protection for maritime trade in war nor effectively deny the use of the seas to Germany's mercantile marine. Further British cruisers from the Second and Third Fleets had to be commissioned on mobilisation and sailed immediately to patrol the focal areas without being given an opportunity for working up into efficient fighting units. Amongst them was the *Carnarvon*, which sailed on 31st July for the Cape Verde area, as flagship of the Fifth Cruiser Squadron, Rear-Admiral A. P. Stoddart, where she was soon joined by the *Cornwall* and the *Cumberland* and (a little later because she happened to be refitting after a commission on the China Station) by the *Monmouth*. Other obsolescent cruisers went to their own war stations, most of them sailing before 4th August; the Eleventh Cruiser Squadron to the west of Ireland; the Twelfth, together with a French force, to the South-Western Approaches; and the Ninth to the Azores; whilst the Sixth, which included the *Good Hope*, went to join the Grand Fleet to replace Cradock's 'Counties'.

One important threat to British trade was removed just before war began. There was time for Berlin to order the *Strassburg* home from the Azores and she passed the *Carnarvon* on the way. But the *Dresden* and the *Karlsrühe*, the latter being a new ship of 4,820 tons, armed with twelve 4·1-inch guns, with a designed speed of 27 knots, were too far afield. The *Dresden* had been watching Germany's interests in Mexico, freely co-operating with both French and British cruisers; but on the 17th July she had sailed for Jamaica, taking ex-President Huerta and his family into exile; and from there she went on to Port au Prince to meet the *Karlsrühe* just out from Germany, to change captains with her on 25th July. Captain Köhler then took the *Karlsrühe* to Havana, whilst Captain Lüdecke went to St Thomas to coal before sailing for home. But on 31st July his orders were amended; Berlin signalled news of the rapidly deteriorating situation in Europe and warned him to be ready to commence cruiser warfare.

The Mexican troubles had brought the whole of Cradock's squadron down to the West Indies, except for the *Lancaster* refitting at Bermuda. So he was at Vera Cruz on 27th July when the Admiralty issued its first war warning; the *Suffolk* was thus well placed to shadow the

Karlsrühe. To deal with the *Dresden,* whose destination after leaving Havana he did not know, Cradock sent the *Berwick* to Jamaica; whilst the *Essex* was ordered to Halifax ready to cover the North Atlantic trade routes, where she would be joined by the *Lancaster.* Lastly, to guard against the German cruisers going south, Cradock proposed to sail the *Bristol* to the Pernambuco area to work with the *Glasgow,* which was visiting Rio de Janeiro. The *Berwick* soon learned that the *Karlsrühe* had reached Havana; but before the British ship could arrive there, Köhler had sailed again to await developments at sea. And when he heard on 3rd August that Germany was at war with France and Russia, he moved to Plana Cays, a deserted anchorage in the Bahamas, intending to lie low until he knew whether Britain would be involved. But since he used his wireless to contact German merchant ships, the *Berwick* knew that her quarry could not be far away. The *Dresden,* on the other hand, was more elusive: reported leaving Port au Prince on 28th July, she was not located again for a fortnight.

Like Jerram, Cradock was not allowed to effect his dispositions without Admiralty intervention. Because they credited the German liners in New York and adjacent ports with an ability to convert themselves into armed merchant cruisers far beyond anything they achieved, the *Good Hope* was diverted from Scapa to Newfoundland, and Stoddart was instructed to send the *Monmouth* to the Pernambuco area, so that the *Bristol* could join the *Essex* until the *Lancaster* should be ready. And the stress which the Admiralty placed on the New York area being the most likely danger spot, persuaded Cradock to take the *Suffolk* north. These movements produced an entirely fortuitous incident. As soon as Köhler heard that Germany was at war with Britain late on 4th August, the *Berwick* then being 400 miles to the south-east of the *Karlsrühe's* position, the German captain sailed to rendezvous with the 25,000 tons *Kronprinz Wilhelm,* 120 miles north of Watling Island. And there, at 1100 on 6th August, Cradock, coming north in the *Suffolk,* sighted both ships. He thought they were coaling: in fact the German cruiser had already transferred two 3·4-inch guns and a third of the ammunition needed to convert the liner into an armed merchant cruiser. And before the more heavily gunned and armoured *Suffolk* could get within range, the enemy vessels parted company, the *Karlsrühe* speeding north, the *Kronprinz Wilhelm* NNE.

Cradock chose the cruiser as his quarry, although the *Suffolk,* limited to 23 knots against the *Karlsrühe's* 27, had small chance of overhauling her; indeed by nightfall the *Karlsrühe* had drawn so far ahead that she was no longer in sight from the *Suffolk*'s bridge. But the British admiral had already wirelessed the northbound *Bristol* to reverse course, and at 2015 Captain B. H. Fanshawe, coming south, sighted the enemy six miles away by the light of a full moon. Quickly swinging his ship on to a parallel course, he surprised his opponent by opening fire at a range of 7,000 yards. Unfortunately, although taken by surprise, Köhler was able to turn his ship away to the east before she suffered damage; and though the engagement continued for a time, spotting conditions were poor, neither vessel securing a hit before the German's greater speed allowed her to draw out of range. Moreover, the stern chase to the south-east which Köhler set the *Bristol*, was soon over: the British cruiser's speed dropped so quickly to 18 knots that by 2230 Fanshawe no longer had his opponent in sight. Yet Köhler had by no means escaped the trap Cradock had set for him. The *Suffolk* had turned to a course designed to intercept the *Karlsrühe*, in the hope that, for lack of coal, the German ship would no longer be able to elude her slower opponents. But the luck which had led Cradock to locate the *Karlsrühe* so soon after the outbreak of war, and the *Bristol* to find her at night, did not remain with the British force; shortly after 0800 next morning the *Suffolk* crossed the *Karlsrühe*'s course just far enough astern for the German vessel to avoid being sighted; and the *Berwick*, which Cradock had also ordered to intercept, chanced to alter course away from her quarry just when she was very close to sighting her. So the *Karlsrühe*, with only 12 tons of coal remaining in her bunkers, reached the safety of Puerto Rico at daybreak on 9th August. Köhler's ship was never again so near to being caught: and Cradock never forgot how the German ship's superior speed enabled her to elude his three cruisers; the incident was to play a part, albeit an unintentional one, in the circumstances which led to his defeat at Coronel.

Having no idea where the *Karlsrühe* had gone, and because the French had sent the *Descartes* and *Condé* to the Caribbean, Cradock saw no reason to change his intention to concentrate most of his ships to the north. But, whilst patrolling off Sandy Hook, he learned that no German liner was at all anxious to put to sea in the guise of an armed merchant cruiser. And on the 13th he heard, first that the *Dresden* had stopped the *Drumcliffe* off the mouth of the Amazon, and then that the *Karlsrühe* was at Curaçao. This changed the whole picture; taking the *Suffolk* into Halifax, he reported that there was no significant threat to Allied trade in the north-west Atlantic. 'The passage across the Atlantic is safe. British trade is running as usual', announced the Admiralty, though patrols would have to be continued against, for example, the threat presented by the *Kronprinz Wilhelm*. But Cradock was not the man to wish to remain in charge of these when there were two German light cruisers near the southern limit of his command. So he obtained Admiralty approval to leave the northern area under the command of the captain of the *Suffolk* and transferred his flag to the *Good Hope*. After his galling failure to catch the *Karlsruhe*, he preferred the larger cruiser's higher speed, despite her age and the rawness of her crew. And in her he sailed for the West Indies on 15th August to join the *Berwick*, *Bristol*, *Condé* and *Descartes*, whose responsibilities were increased by the opening of the Panama Canal. He reached St Lucia on the 23rd.

Where were the German cruisers now, and, more important, what were Köhler's and Lüdecke's intentions? The *Dresden* had orders to work her way down the coast of South America where there were many out-of-the-way bays in which she might hide and coal from her tender, the *Baden*, and to operate against British shipping in the Pernambuco area, before proceeding further south to the even more profitable region of the Plate. The *Karlsruhe*, on the other hand, having been deterred from venturing north, proposed to raid British and French ports in the West Indies; but she could not obtain sufficient coal at Puerto Rico and was forced to go south to the Dutch island of Curaçao for it. This led Köhler to the Pernambuco area, and by 21st August reports of sinkings and sightings of both German cruisers off the South American coast led the Admiralty to appreciate that there was a major threat to British trade in an area where there were only the *Glasgow* and the recently arrived *Monmouth*. Moreover, Admiral Stoddart, within whose command the Pernambuco area came, was too busy in the Cape Verde region to do more than send the *Cornwall* as reinforcement, though the Admiralty added the armed merchant cruisers *Otranto* and *Macedonia*. Cradock was therefore ordered to extend his operations beyond the southern limits of his own command—the genesis of his fateful move into South American waters.

There is no need to detail the operations of the British ships during the next couple of weeks as they searched for an elusive enemy, nor to follow every move of the *Karlsruhe* in the Pernambuco area and of the *Dresden* as she cruised further south. On 3rd September Cradock signalled the Admiralty (*to facilitate subsequent reference, this and other signals in this chapter are numbered serially in parentheses*):

Good Hope arrived Fernando Noronha, visiting St Paul's Rocks, and will arrive Pernambuco 5th September for orders. *Cornwall* is in wireless touch proceeding south. *Glasgow* reports proceeding with *Monmouth* and *Otranto* to Magellan Straits, where number of German ships reported, presumably colliers, and where concentration of German cruisers from China, Pacific Ocean and Atlantic Ocean appears possible. (*No. 1*)

The Admiralty, who had not accepted a memorandum prepared by the Assistant Director of the Operations Division, Captain (later Admiral Sir Herbert) Richmond *in mid-August* proposing the dispatch of three, or better still four armoured cruisers to the *west* coast of South America to meet the likelihood of von Spee appearing in that area, replied:

> You are to remain and take charge of the SE Coast of America Station. Ships under your orders: *Good Hope, Berwick, Bristol, Glasgow, Monmouth,* (and A.M.C.'s) *Carmania, Otranto, Victorian.* . . . (*No. 2*)

Cradock, understandably concerned with the possibility of meeting more than the *Dresden* and *Karlsrühe*, responded to this on 5th September with a further signal:

> *Gneisenau* and *Scharnhorst* reported Caroline Islands. . . . 8th August. Is there any later information as to movements? Several German colliers said to be in vicinity of Magellan Straits. . . . (*No. 3*)

The Admiralty could only tell him:

> No certain information of these ships since 8th August. . . . Magellan Straits and its vicinity quite possible. Falkland Islands anchorages might also be used by them. (*No. 4*)

On the basis of this intelligence, and the need to guard against the elusive *Dresden*, Cradock ordered the *Good Hope, Cornwall, Carmania, Macedonia* and *Bristol* to operate between the Abrolhos Rocks and the Plate, and sent Luce with the *Glasgow, Monmouth* and *Otranto* to the Magellan Straits to prevent the *Dresden* entering the Pacific. Four days later, 14th September, these dispositions met with success: the *Carmania* found the liner *Cap Trafalgar*, which had been armed by the gunboat *Eber*, coaling off the Brazilian island of Trinidada and sank her after a spirited action lasting an hour and a half, though the *Carmania* was herself so seriously damaged that she had to be escorted by the *Macedonia* to Gibraltar for repairs.

Against this, the *Dresden* continued to elude the British squadron. She sank the *Holmwood*, carrying 6,000 tons of coal, off the Plate on 26th

August; news of this was stale by nearly a week by the time it reached Cradock, but it was enough for him to make a further move towards disaster. He took the *Good Hope* south to support Luce's force, and they met near Santa Catherina, on 14th September as a result of a false report that the *Dresden* was coaling there. Lüdecke, however, showed no talent for cruiser warfare; he had already abandoned the Plate area and, by 31st August, moved so far south as Gayetano Bay on the Patagonian coast. Thence he headed for Orange Bay in the Magellan Straits, where he arrived on 4th September after weathering a severe storm; and on the 8th Berlin signalled him: 'It is advisable to operate with the *Leipzig*', which Lüdecke knew to be on the Pacific coast. The arrival of the supply ship *Santa Isabel* on the 12th with false news that British cruisers were already off the eastern entrance to the Magellan Straits, coupled with Berlin's injunction, was enough to persuade the German captain to proceed into the Pacific which he entered on 18th September.

Meantime, the continued absence of firm news of von Spee and the repeated suggestions from Jerram and Patey, together with further intelligence reports from South America, had led the Admiralty seriously to consider the situation which would arise if the German squadron was coming across the Pacific. As a result they signalled Cradock on 14th September:

> There is a strong probability of *Scharnhorst* and *Gneisenau* arriving in the Magellan Straits or on the west coast of South America. The Germans have begun to carry on trade on the west coast of South America. Leave sufficient force to deal with *Dresden* and *Karlsrühe*. Concentrate a squadron strong enough to meet *Scharnhorst* and *Gneisenau*, making Falkland Islands your coaling base. *Canopus* is now en route to Abrolhos, *Defence* is joining you from Mediterranean. Until *Defence* joins, keep at least *Canopus* and one 'County' class with your flagship. As soon as you have superior force, search the Magellan Straits with squadron, being ready to return and cover the River Plate or, according to information, search north as far as Valparaiso. Break up the German trade and destroy the German cruisers. . . . (*No. 5*)

This and other signals are quoted almost in full because in them lies the answer to the problem posed at the end of Chapter 1; whether Cradock, in the light of the instructions he received from the Admiralty, was justified in engaging von Spee off Coronel on 1st November. Two points about this one will be noted. First, its confused phrasing; could Cradock be sure that he understood Their Lordships' intentions? Secondly, he was specifically told that the old cruisers *Good Hope* and

Monmouth and the obsolete battleship *Canopus* were a superior force to von Spee's crack ships, the *Scharnhorst* and *Gneisenau*. This was not, however, the unanimous opinion of the Naval War Staff. A memorandum dated 7th September had recommended reinforcing Cradock with three armoured cruisers and a light cruiser from the eastern Mediterranean and Red Sea. Though the threat to our troop convoys in the Indian Ocean presented by the *Emden* and *Königsberg* prevented Battenberg and Vice-Admiral Sturdee, the Chief of Staff, from accepting this recommendation, they proposed instead to send battle-cruisers from the Grand Fleet. But Churchill would not agree to over-rule Jellicoe's strong protests against a reduction in his capital ship strength. So it was decided to send only one armoured cruiser, the *Defence*, from the Mediterranean. Though no more than a compromise solution, she was a ship of 14,600 tons completed in 1908, with the heavy armament of four 9·2-inch and ten 7·5-inch guns, and a speed of 23 knots, two features that made her a more powerful vessel for Cradock's purpose than the *Canopus* or any other ship under his command.

Any doubts Cradock may have had as to how he should implement his instructions were, however, dissipated two days later by von Spee's appearance off Apia. And since Samoa is 2,500 miles nearer South America than Ponapé, the receipt of this news at the Admiralty should have strengthened their decision to reinforce Cradock. But, on the basis of a report that von Spee had left Apia in a north-*westerly* direction, they signalled Cradock on the 16th:

> Situation changed. *Scharnhorst* and *Gneisenau* appeared off Samoa on 14th September . . . and left steering NW. . . . German trade on west coast of America is to be attacked at once. . . . Cruisers need not be concentrated. Two cruisers and an armed liner would appear sufficient for Magellan Straits and west coast. Report what you propose about *Canopus*. . . . (*No. 6*)

Cradock, who could reasonably assume that the Admiralty had more intelligence about von Spee's intentions than were included in this signal, replied from Montevideo on 18th September:

> When finished coaling am proceeding with *Good Hope, Glasgow, Monmouth* and *Otranto* to sweep south, region of Magellan Straits, and search. *Glasgow* and *Monmouth* will continue to west coast . . . to destroy trade. *Canopus* will be ordered . . . to Rio de la Plata to guard trade and colliers and remain pending events. (*No. 7*)

79

The Admiralty's new instructions to Cradock were not, in fact, to be of great consequence to the future. But they made another more vital decision on the basis of their false appreciation: the *Defence* was ordered to remain at Malta, and Cradock was *not* informed that she would *not*, after all, be joining his command.

Following the entry of Japan into the war, when all von Spee's sources of intelligence indicated that the Allied navies were searching for him to the north and west, the German admiral had sailed his armoured cruisers with five supply ships for Christmas Island, an uninhabited atoll 1,800 miles to the east of the Marshall Islands. Meantime the *Nürnberg* went to Honolulu, where von Schönberg had some difficulty in persuading the American authorities to allow his ship to coal, and was then sent to Fanning Island to destroy the British cable between Fiji and Honolulu. He rejoined the squadron at Christmas Island, where the armoured cruisers coaled, with the news that a New Zealand force had occupied Samoa, whereupon von Spee decided to make this German colony his next objective. 'The forces in occupation will need constant provisioning by steamers and these will be protected', he wrote; 'it may therefore be presumed that steamers and warships are lying off Apia. An attack before dawn on ships at anchor might have good results.' He was willing to risk the possibility that the *Australia* might be there. But when the two armoured cruisers approached Apia at 0300 on 14th September with guns manned, they found nothing larger than a sailing vessel in the port. Having insufficient men to attempt a landing, and seeing no bombardment target worth the expenditure of irreplaceable ammunition, von Spee withdrew, initially steering a north-westerly course so as to deceive the island's observers. How well this feint would affect the future he could not know.

The Asiatic Squadron's next port of call was the isolated British Suvarov Island, 500 miles to the east; but, finding that the swell prevented coaling, they went 700 miles further on to Bora Bora in the well-cultivated Society Islands, a welcome change from the coral atolls they had previously visited. The few French inhabitants deemed it wisest to offer no resistance whilst the German vessels coaled and landed men to obtain supplies on 21st September. Von Spee needed, however, more than he found at Bora Bora, so he went on to Papieté, the capital of Tahiti, only 150 miles away. 'I intend to engage any enemy ships encountered at Tahiti and to requisition coal and provisions', he signalled his squadron; 'a parley boat will be sent and will return: the ships will follow a little later. Force will be used if our demands are refused. Our first objectives will be the points from which fire is opened, then defences, the arsenal, public buildings, etc. . . . Armed cutters are to be available to carry requisitioned goods. . . .' But when the *Scharnhorst* and *Gneisenau* approached the island at dawn on the 22nd, it was evident that the French Governor intended to resist a landing. So the German ships opened fire on the fort and on the old gunboat *Zelée*, which was abandoned by her crew. The Governor responded by igniting the stock of coal and blowing up the storehouses. Then von Spee found that the leading marks indicating the course for entering the harbour had been removed and decided it would be too hazardous to proceed further with his plans. So, once again, he achieved practically nothing at the expense of irreplaceable ammunition and of disclosing his movements to the Allies. For the French hastily sent a steamer to Samoa with news of the attack, whence it reached London on 30th September.

Notwithstanding this fresh evidence that von Spee was moving east, the Admiralty continued to guard against his going west. Though Churchill recorded his reaction as: 'At any rate for several weeks we need not worry about their ships', they signalled Patey in Australian waters:

> It is very probable that *Gneisenau* and *Scharnhorst* may repeat attacks similar to the one at Papieté, therefore they may be expected to return towards Samoa, Fiji or even New Zealand. Making Suva your base search for these cruisers in these waters. . . . (*No. 8*)

To Cradock they only signalled the bare facts:

> Governor of Papieté reports that *Gneisenau* and *Scharnhorst* arrived at Papieté 22nd September with two colliers. They sank gunboat *Zelée* and destroyed half the town by shell fire. They left the same morning steaming NE. (*No. 9*)

We cannot, however, know Cradock's reaction to this message because it never reached the *Good Hope*. He left the Plate area on 22nd September, together with the *Monmouth*, *Glasgow* and *Otranto*, believing his task to be that detailed in signal *No. 6*, to attack German trade in the Pacific and to search for the *Dresden*, the only enemy warship he was likely to meet.

From Tahiti von Spee took his squadron another 850 miles towards victory. From 26th September to 3rd October he was at Nukuhiva in the French Marquesas Islands. Since these had no communication with the outside world except by sea, the Germans were able to coal in safety and obtain fresh provisions from the Société Commercial d'Oceanie, a German firm of long standing in the Pacific. And whilst the ships rested their engines, their crews were, for the first time for two months, able to go ashore, von Spee paying a courtesy visit to the Roman Catholic mission. He then sent two of his supply ships off to Honolulu with duplicate copies of important dispatches to Berlin reporting his intention to proceed by way of Easter Island and Juan Fernandez to Valparaiso, and to the German consul-general at San Francisco stating his coal requirements at these places. Finally, and perhaps most important of all, the *Scharnhorst* heard the *Dresden* communicating with the *Leipzig* by wireless, so that von Spee learned for the first time that both these light cruisers were off the west coast of South America.

Since leaving the Magellan Straits on 18th September, the *Dresden* had steamed up the Pacific coast to Coronel, entering that port on the 25th, where the German consul told him of the expected arrival of von Spee in Chilean waters at the end of October. This news, coupled with a report that the *Good Hope*, *Monmouth*, *Glasgow* and *Otranto* had passed through the Straits of Magellan on 28th September, sent Lüdecke north to coal at Mas a Fuera, from where, on the night of 2nd/3rd October, he established wireless touch with the *Leipzig*.

At the beginning of August Captain Haun's ship was protecting German interests on the west coast of Mexico. On the 2nd, hearing that hostilities in Europe were imminent, he left Mazatlan, accompanied by a collier, to rejoin von Spee at Tsingtau. But when war began he realised this was not practicable and decided instead to operate off San Francisco against British shipping running north to Vancouver, and perhaps attack the only British warships in the area, the obsolete cruiser *Rainbow* and the sloops *Algerine* and *Shearwater*. The *Leipzig* was consequently off the Golden Gate from 11th to 18th August. But she achieved nothing, whilst the *Rainbow* escorted the two British sloops safely from Mexican waters to Vancouver and thereafter, in view of her age, avoided action with a modern adversary. British merchant shipping, in accordance with orders from London, remained in harbour. This was not all: the headquarters of the highly efficient German naval attaché, Captain Boy-Ed, were too far away for him to prevent the

American authorities placing such a strict interpretation on International Law that Haun found it very difficult to obtain enough coal. There was news, too, that the *Newcastle* was on her way from Hong Kong; and if Japan entered the war, there would be the armoured cruiser *Idzumo* to contend with. So the *Leipzig* began to move south, coaling at Ballenas Bay in Lower California on 27th August, a decision confirmed by a signal from Berlin dated 3rd September: 'Transfer cruiser warfare to south-west America and the Atlantic.'

On 11th September Haun scored his first success by sinking the *Elsinore* in ballast on the route to Panama. On the 18th he reached the Galapagos Islands. On the 25th he sank the *Bankfields* carrying a cargo of sugar to Panama for Britain. By the 28th he was off the Peruvian coast. But whilst Haun was now obtaining coal without difficulty, he found the trade routes devoid of British shipping which was, wisely, detained in port. So, when on 1st October he received Berlin's order to operate with the *Dresden*, and the already mentioned inaccurate news of Cradock's passage of the Magellan Straits, he decided to make for Easter Island. Since he had no news of von Spee's plans this was a curious coincidence: but its wisdom was confirmed on the night of 2nd/3rd October when he heard from the *Dresden*: 'My position Mas a Fuera Island. Intend to proceed to Easter Island to get into touch with the Cruiser Squadron.' When the *Scharnhorst* then managed to establish communication with the *Dresden* on the night of 5th/6th October, von Spee was able to co-ordinate the arrival of these reinforcements for his squadron at this isolated island in the Pacific. Such was the way in which both the *Leipzig* and the *Dresden* joined von Spee in the middle of October, bringing the strength of his squadron up to five ships, two armoured and three light cruisers. And from Lüdecke the German admiral learned the limited strength of the Allied forces believed to be on the west coast of America; the *Idzumo* and *Newcastle* to the north; the *Good Hope*, *Monmouth*, *Glasgow* and *Otranto* to the south. This encouraged him to write to his wife: 'Things appear favourable enough: anyway they are better than before.'

It will be convenient to record the German squadron's movements up to the morning of 1st November before relating the circumstances in which, contrary to his signal No. 7, Cradock took the *Good Hope* and *Otranto* into the Pacific instead of sending only the *Glasgow* and *Monmouth*. Von Spee was at isolated Easter Island from 12th to 18th October where, after again coaling from three supply ships, he obtained fresh meat from an English cattle ranch, whose owner knew nothing of the outbreak of a world war. And again the German crews were able to go ashore, von Spee taking his son Otto to look at the island's grotesque statues, long fallen from their monolithic platforms. Another 1,500 miles steaming and on 26th October the German squadron reached Mas a Fuera, a desolate rock that provided a sheltered anchorage, where von Spee was unexpectedly joined by the A.M.C. *Prinz Eitel Friedrich*, which had had to abandon attempts to attack trade in Australian waters because she could not obtain adequate coal supplies there. (For the same reason the *Cormoran* had to seek internment at Guam.) But there was insufficient coal to fill this vessel's bunkers as well as those of his cruisers, a factor which caused von Spee considerable anxiety since he now expected to meet Cradock's force at any time. So, when he moved on to sight the Andes on 30th October, he sent the *Prinz Eitel* with his supply ships into Valparaiso and Coronel—whereby as recorded in Chapter 1, von Spee learned of the *Glasgow*'s arrival at the latter port on 31st October, and decided to close the place in the hope of trapping her there.

Three months of war had passed and the German cruisers had steamed some 10,000 miles, for the most part in tropical heat, with little technical trouble; and von Spee had managed to keep his ships supplied despite the Allies' command of the sea, the health and morale of their crews remaining excellent despite the strain of war watch-keeping and the uncertainty of what the future had in store for them. They had, however, done neither significant military damage nor (the operations of the *Emden* excepted) interrupted Allied maritime trade to any appreciable extent.

Meanwhile Cradock in the *Good Hope*, with the *Monmouth*, *Glasgow* and *Otranto* in company, had been steaming down the eastern side of South America. On the 22nd, having coaled on English Bank, he left to search for the *Dresden* in the many bays that indent the coast to the south of the Plate; and on the 25th he chanced to meet the Pacific Steam Navigation Company's *Ortega*. From her he received dramatic news: on the 18th, the day the *Dresden* passed into the Pacific, the British liner, carrying 500 French reservists, had been chased by the German cruiser, only escaping her by entering neutral waters. Cradock at once set course for the Magellan Straits, arriving at the substantial Chilean port of Punta Arenas on the 28th. There the British consul told him that the *Dresden* had been using Orange Bay, a small harbour lying amidst the snows and glaciers of Hoste Island. In the hope that she might have returned there, possibly accompanied by the *Leipzig* and *Nürnberg*, the British admiral sailed his squadron after midnight without lights so that its departure would not be observed by the considerable German colony, and threaded the difficult Cockburn Channel in thick weather and falling snow to round Cape Horn and enter the broad reaches of Nassau Bay. Thence his ships closed the hideout of their quarry. 'Battle of Orange Bay was rather a farce,' recorded one of the *Glasgow*'s officers, 'as the enemy didn't turn up.' Since the British squadron now needed coal, Cradock sent the *Otranto* back to Punta Arenas and took his three cruisers to the Falkland Islands. The *Glasgow* and *Monmouth* sailed again on 3rd October to pick up the *Otranto* and to comply with the Admiralty's orders to operate against German trade on the west coast. The *Good Hope* remained at the Falklands against the possibility of the *Dresden* coming east again, Cradock having no further news of von Spee since that contained in signal *No. 6*.

This chapter has been so much concerned with the movements of many ships, chiefly British and German, that it is easy to regard them as pawns upon a chessboard, or as puppets manipulated by the admirals and captains who commanded them. But these men were human; upon them fell the lonely load of responsibility of deciding the movements of their ships upon which so much depended. And they had always to remember their crews without which their ships were nothing. Their physical health and happiness, as well as discipline, had to be maintained under many difficulties. Coaling, for example, which in war had to be done every 7–10 days, 'is one of the things in a modern ship of war that seems very primitive,' wrote an officer of the *Good Hope* in his diary. 'The bags in the collier are filled by hand, hoisted onboard by derricks, and then carried again by hand on a wheelbarrow to the various small openings on deck. Everything and everybody gets covered in a fine, almost impalpable coal dust. . . . We coal all day. Everything is dirty and one feels miserably uncomfortable. As all the officers have got absolutely black faces it's difficult to distinguish one from another. . . .' Again: 'Having no refrigerators we grew to loathe corned beef and very soon our supply of potatoes failed and we had to resort to rice. Then our flour got mouldy and bread was rather sour. Perhaps the worst of all was the millions of cockroaches which inhabited the ship.' There was also the enervating effect of tropical heat in ill-ventilated ships lacking any form of air-conditioning, and the consequent maddening irritation of prickly-heat from which all but a fortunate few suffered.

Mails, too, were rare and long delayed in bringing news from home. And concert parties and deck-hockey, though they did much to keep up the spirits of officers and men, were no substitute for shore leave which could so seldom be granted that it involved its own problems. 'General leave is given to the crew. A large number get hopelessly drunk ashore. In coming off in the evening twenty fell into the water and were nearly drowned. . . . Captain issued an order warning all of the penalties [to which] they are liable for rendering themselves unfit for duty.'

Whilst at Punta Arenas the *Otranto* intercepted German wireless messages which led Cradock to leave the Falklands at high speed on 5th October and to order Luce to rejoin him for another descent on Orange Bay. But, noted one of the *Glasgow*'s officers: 'Second Battle of Orange Bay also a frost. Weather atrocious and it would have been quite impossible to fight our guns. Rather interesting if we met an enemy light cruiser in similar conditions.' 'A frost' is not, however, the right word: the *Good Hope* found a noticeboard ashore bearing the name *Bremen*, a ship that had surveyed the bay in 1912; and pencil marks on the board indicating that the *Dresden* had been there on 9th, 10th and 11th September. So Luce's ships reversed course to the westward: 'it blew, snowed, hailed and sleeted as hard as it is possible to do,' wrote one of their officers; '*Monmouth* was rolling thirty-five degrees at times and . . . was practically a submarine. We finally got past caring what might happen—what with the weather, strain, and extreme cold.'

The *Good Hope* returned to the Falkland Islands where, on 7th October, Cradock received a message sent by the Admiralty two days earlier which entirely changed the situation. On the 4th Suva wireless station had intercepted a message from the *Scharnhorst* to the effect that she was on the way from the Marquesas to Easter Island, from which

> . . . it appears that *Scharnhorst* and *Gneisenau* are working across to South America. You must be prepared to have to meet them in company, possibly with a *Dresden* scouting for them. *Canopus* should accompany *Glasgow*, *Monmouth* and *Otranto*, the ships to search and protect trade in combination. . . . If you propose *Good Hope* to go, leave *Monmouth* on east coast. . . . (*No. 10*)

Cradock replied next day with additional intelligence and his intentions:

. . . Indications show possibility of *Dresden, Leipzig, Nürnberg* joining *Gneisenau* and *Scharnhorst*. Have ordered *Canopus* to Falkland Islands where I intend to concentrate and avoid division of forces. Have ordered *Glasgow, Monmouth* and *Otranto* not to go north of Valparaiso until German cruisers are again located. *Karlsrühe* apparently operating in South American waters: suggest therefore *Essex* be now detached and relieve *Cornwall*. . . . *Cornwall* then proceeding south. With reference to your [*No. 6*] does *Defence* join my command? Do regulations of Panama Canal Company permit passage of belligerent ships at present time? (*No. 11*)

Since this signal was not received at the Admiralty until the 12th, it was dealt with there at the same time as another sent by Cradock on the 11th after further consideration of the problem presented by the approach of von Spee's squadron:

Without alarming, respectfully suggest that in event of the enemy's heavy cruisers and others concentrating west coast of South America, it is necessary to have a British force on each coast strong enough to bring them into action. For otherwise should the concentrated British force sent from south-east coast be evaded in the Pacific . . . and get behind the enemy, the latter could destroy Falklands, English Bank and Abrolhos coaling bases in turn, with little to stop them, and with British ships unable to follow up owing to want of coal, enemy might possibly reach West Indies. (*No. 12*)

It is undeniable that these signals were lacking in clarity. Did Cradock mean that he was concentrating his *whole* force at the Falklands; or was he intending that the *Monmouth, Glasgow* and *Otranto* should operate on the west coast whilst the *Good Hope, Canopus, Cornwall,* and perhaps the *Defence,* constituted another force on the south-east coast? If the latter, Luce's three ships were clearly no match for the Germans. On the other hand, Cradock's second signal (*No. 12*) referred to the concentrated British force being evaded in the Pacific. So Churchill minuted his copy of the signal to Battenberg:

It would be best for the British ships to keep within supporting distance of one another, whether in the Straits or near the Falklands, and to postpone the cruise along the west coast until the present uncertainty about *Scharnhorst–Gneisenau* is cleared up. They and not the trade are our quarry for the moment. Above all we must not miss them.

But the First Sea Lord was satisfied that this was Cradock's intention: 'Settled' was his brief reply to the First Lord.

Two days later, however, Churchill and Battenberg discussed the situation, and the former subsequently minuted:

> I understand from our conversation that the dispositions you proposed for the South Pacific and South Atlantic were as follows: (1) Cradock to concentrate at the Falklands *Canopus, Monmouth, Good Hope* and *Otranto*. (2) To send *Glasgow* round to look for *Leipzig* and attack and protect trade on the west coast of South America as far north as Valparaiso. (3) *Defence* to join *Carnarvon* in forming a new combat squadron on the great trade route from Rio. . . . These arrangements have my full approval. . . . I presume Cradock is fully aware of the possibility of *Scharnhorst* and *Gneisenau* arriving on or after the 17th instant in his neighbourhood; and that if not strong enough to attack, he will do his utmost to shadow them, pending the arrival of reinforcements.

But the reply then sent to Cradock in answer to both his messages said no more than this:

> Your concentration of *Good Hope, Canopus, Monmouth, Glasgow* and *Otranto* for combined operations concurred in. Stoddart in *Carnarvon* has been ordered to Montevideo. . . . *Defence* ordered to join *Carnarvon*. He will also have *Cornwall, Bristol, Macedonia* and *Orama* under his orders. *Essex* remains in West Indies. . . . (*No. 13*)

The same day the Admiralty signalled Stoddart at Sierra Leone:

> Proceed down trade route to Montevideo, calling at Pernambuco on the way. *Defence* is following you from Gibraltar. . . . *Cornwall, Bristol, Macedonia* and *Orama* will be under your orders. Keep sufficient force ready to concentrate in case German squadron from Pacific escape past Cradock who has *Good Hope, Canopus, Monmouth, Glasgow* and *Otranto*. . . . He is now in vicinity of Falkland Islands. (*No. 14*)

The signal to Cradock referred to 'combined operations' but made no reference to concentrating his force in the Falkland Islands area. Unlike Churchill, the Naval War Staff assumed that this was implicit in Cradock's *No. 11*: he had, in fact, allowed the *Monmouth, Glasgow* and *Otranto* to go round to the west coast, whilst the *Good Hope* awaited the *Canopus* at Port Stanley, the capital of the Falklands.

> The *Good Hope* was here for some time before she went to find these swine [wrote the Governor's A.D.C.]. The Admiral was a very brave old man; he knew that he was going to almost certain death in fighting these new and powerful ships and it seemed to be quite all right as far as he was concerned. . . . I was dining with him one night and about the only thing I could find in his cabin was a piece of old Cloisonnée with

16 *First Sea Lord from 1912 until a few days before Coronel: Admiral of the Fleet Prince Louis of Battenberg*

17 *First Lord of the Admiralty at the time of Coronel and the Falklands: Winston Churchill inspecting a naval camp in 1914*

18 '*A veritable dynamo*': *Admiral of the Fleet Lord Fisher, First Sea Lord from a few days before Coronel until the summer of 1915*
From a painting by H. von Herkomer

the top knocked off. I asked him how it got broken and he said, 'I got that in China when I was a lieutenant and I have carried it with me ever since and it has always brought me luck, but last month when we changed over into this ship from the *Suffolk* at half an hour's notice, I only managed to get on board with my dog in one fist and this vase in the other; and carrying Cloisonnée vases from one ship to another in mid-ocean isn't any fun, and I dropped this as soon as I got on to the *Good Hope* and knocked its head off, and I'm very much afraid that that means I am not going to see those Germans at all.'

But when the *Canopus* arrived on 18th October, Cradock learned that she needed five days in harbour to repair machinery defects and clean boilers. At the same time he was misinformed by Captain Grant, for a reason explained in Chapter 1, that the old battleship's speed was restricted to 12 knots. So on the 18th he signalled the Admiralty:

> *Karlsrühe* not reported since 22nd September. Consider it possible . . . that she has been driven west [of Cape Horn] and is to join other five [von Spee's force]. I fear that strategically the speed of my squadron cannot exceed 12 knots, owing to *Canopus*, but shall trust circumstances will enable me to force an action. (*No. 15*)

In fact the *Karlsrühe* was operating in the Pernambuco area, but the Admiralty did not relieve one of Cradock's anxieties by telling him this, any more than they answered his question about belligerent warships passing through the Panama Canal. (The Foreign Office was having difficulty in getting the State Department to give a clear decision about this, though it seemed that they would agree to a maximum of three at any one time, enough for the *Scharnhorst* and *Gneisenau* to descend on the West Indies.)

To Churchill Cradock's signal was confirmation that he understood the Admiralty's intention that his force should be concentrated on the Falklands. Accepting the doubtful proposition that the obsolete *Canopus* gave the old cruisers *Good Hope* and *Monmouth* the strength to deal with von Spee's two crack cruisers, all seemed well. But in writing a last letter to the Governor of the Falklands, thanking him for his hospitality, Cradock said:

> I shall not fail to let them know at home officially what I have seen and think of your gallant precautions and plan for upholding our honour [against attack by von Spee]. Would that all our dependencies were the same. . . . I will give all warning I can if the squadron 'from Germany' eludes us; and only in case of my 'disappearance' will you send the letter

to Meux. I mean to say, if my squadron disappears—and me too—completely. I have no intention after forty years at sea of being an unheard victim. . . .

The letter to Admiral Meux has not been traced, but we may surmise that Cradock said he supposed it to be his duty to seek out von Spee in the Pacific even though he had been given insufficient force to ensure victory. For the Governor's A.D.C. wrote:

> He knew what he was up against and asked for a fast cruiser with big guns to be added to his squadron for he had nothing very powerful and nothing very fast, but the Admiralty said he'd have to go without, so old Cradock said 'All right; we'll do without', and he slipped off quietly early one morning and left the *Canopus* to look after the colliers and transports and picked up the *Glasgow* and the *Monmouth* and set out to look for these crack Germans.

Well might the poet say:

> . . . *he understates*
> *His peril in reporting to Whitehall*
> *And merely hints what he should bluntly say*
> *In forceful language to a busy staff.*

for on 24th October Cradock only signalled:

> *Good Hope* left [Port Stanley] 22nd October via Cape Horn. *Canopus* followed on 23rd October via Magellan Straits [with three colliers] for west coast of South America. (*No. 16*)

Whilst this told the Admiralty that, contrary to their instructions, Cradock was taking his whole force into the Pacific, they could suppose that he intended both the *Good Hope* and *Canopus* to join Luce's ships. And since Stoddart's squadron, now concentrating north of Montevideo, could be used against von Spee should he elude Cradock and enter the Atlantic, they saw no reason to intervene.

On 27th October the *Good Hope* reached Vallenar Roads, when the *Canopus* had progressed no further than Punta Arenas. And, whilst coaling, Cradock signalled the Admiralty again:

> With reference to orders in [signal *No. 10*] to search for enemy and our great desire for early success, consider it impracticable on account of *Canopus*'s slow speed, to find and destroy enemy's squadron. Consequently have ordered *Defence* to join me after calling at Montevideo for orders. *Canopus* will be employed on necessary convoying of colliers.

From experience of 6th August most respectfully submit not to oppose depredations of *Karlsrühe*. May it continue until he meets vessel of superior speed. (*No. 17*)

Since Churchill was now gravely preoccupied with another matter, he did no more than minute: 'This telegram is very obscure and I do not understand what Cradock intends or wishes'. But to the Naval War Staff it should have been clear that Cradock did not consider it possible to locate and destroy von Spee if his squadron was tied to the *Canopus*, and that he had therefore ordered the *Defence* to join him. Having had no news of this armoured cruiser since 14th September when the Admiralty first ordered her to South America, he assumed that she was by now on the east coast. The wording of Cradock's last two sentences did not, however, help the Admiralty to understand him. Recalling, from the galling way in which the *Karlsrühe* had eluded him, the vital importance of speed for catching the German cruiser, he meant to imply that it was useless to employ the *Defence* to hunt for the *Karlsrühe* in the Atlantic. But the Admiralty was much too busy to interpret such oblique references; they assumed there must have been a cipher error.

The Naval War Staff's consequent appreciation was summed up in a minute to the First Sea Lord dated 29th October:

> The situation on the West Coast seems safe. If *Gneisenau* and *Scharnhorst* have gone north they will meet eventually *Idzumo*, *Newcastle* and *Hizen* [a Japanese battleship which was on her way to the west coast of North America] moving south, and will be forced south on *Glasgow* and *Monmouth* who have good speed and can keep touch and draw them south on to *Good Hope* and *Canopus*, who should keep within supporting distance of each other.

So Cradock's orders to the *Defence* were countermanded when Stoddart represented that without her he would have insufficient force to meet von Spee in the Atlantic, a decision signalled to Cradock:

> *Defence* is to remain on east coast under orders of Stoddart. This will leave sufficient force on each side in case the hostile cruisers appear there on the trade route. Japanese battleship *Hizen* shortly expected on North American coast. She will join Japanese *Idzumo* and *Newcastle* and move south towards the Galapagos. (*No. 18*)

But this message, more especially its vital first sentence, did not reach the *Good Hope* until after noon on 1st November, when the *Glasgow* brought it out from Coronel. And by then Cradock was too far committed to his search for the *Leipzig* to consider any change in his immediate plans which were to lead to his death soon after the sun set that evening.

Before analysing, from all this evidence, 'the reason why' for the disaster off Coronel, the action taken on 3rd November, *before* news of the battle reached London should be noted. A telegram from the British consul-general at Valparaiso reported that von Spee's squadron had been located close off the Chilean coast on 1st November as the result of stopping a Chilean merchant ship, whereupon the Admiralty signalled Cradock:

> *Defence* has been ordered to join your flag with all dispatch. *Glasgow* should keep in touch with the enemy. You should keep in touch with *Glasgow* concentrating the rest of your squadron including *Canopus*. It is important that you should effect your junction with *Defence* at earliest possible moment subject to keeping touch with enemy. . . . (*No. 19*)

But in the First Lord's words: 'We were already talking to the void.'

Churchill also wrote less than a decade later: 'I cannot accept for the Admiralty any share in the responsibility' for this disaster for British arms. This can have only one interpretation; that the whole responsibility was Cradock's. That the admiral must bear his share was made clear in Chapter 1: but can the First Lord's larger verdict be upheld, or was it a grave injustice to the name of a brave man?

From as early as 17th August the two 'men on the spot' chiefly concerned, Jerram and Patey, repeatedly told the Admiralty that the most likely destination of the German armoured cruisers, whose whereabouts during the first five weeks of the war could only be assessed as somewhere in the western Pacific, was South America. Yet, although on 23rd August the Admiralty decreed that 'the destruction of *Scharnhorst* and *Gneisenau* is of the first importance', no priority was given to this object. Because it was *possible* that von Spee *might* attack trade in Far East waters, where it was of greater value than on the west coast of South America, Jerram was ordered to deploy his ships for its protection (except the *Newcastle*). And because the British Government encouraged Australia and New Zealand to launch early attacks on Germany's defenceless island colonies, whose capture could have been undertaken later with no inconvenience to the Allied cause, Patey's ships, including the battle-cruiser *Australia*, had to protect these seaborne expeditions. Nothing was left to be moved eastwards.

Cradock, however, was moving down the *east* coast of South America, seeking the *Karlsrühe* and *Dresden*; and on 6th September the Admiralty, in reply to a query from the admiral, conceded that the Magellan Straits and the Falkland Islands might be von Spee's destination (signals *Nos. 3 and 4*). They then considered the adequacy of Cradock's squadron to meet this threat and sent him detailed instructions on 14th September (signal *No. 5*). In stressing the need to meet the enemy with superior strength, the Admiralty reiterated an accepted principle of war. They realised Cradock did not have this strength and considered reinforcing him with three armoured cruisers, but whittled this down to one. The *Good Hope*, *Monmouth* and *Defence* might have been an adequate force; but the *Scharnhorst* and *Gneisenau* could reach South American waters before the *Defence*; so the Admiralty told Cradock to keep the *Canopus* with the *Good Hope* and *Monmouth*. Nothing in signal *No. 5* indicated, however, that the Admiralty realised that the battleship's slow speed, even if this had been 17 knots, made it impracticable for Cradock to comply with their order 'to destroy the [much faster] German cruisers'. Nor, on the other hand, did they say that, until the *Defence* joined, Cradock was to confine himself to searching for the *Scharnhorst* and *Gneisenau*, using the *Canopus* to deter von Spee from accepting battle with the older, under-gunned, newly commissioned *Good Hope* and *Monmouth*.

The Admiralty's confused, unrealistic and, consequently, misleading instructions had, however, no sooner been sent than von Spee was at last located off Samoa, when, coincidentally, the *Emden* began her marauding career in the Bay of Bengal. Against the latter some of Jerram's ships had to be sent into the Indian Ocean; the rest went to strengthen the escort of the first Australia–New Zealand convoy, which could not be delayed since the troops were urgently required in France. But now the Admiralty rejected all the evidence that indicated von Spee's true destination: they allowed the powerful Japanese Fleet to continue its largely useless patrols among the western Pacific islands; they acceded to pressure from the New Zealand Government to add the *Australia* to the troop convoy's escort when this powerful ship might have been sent in pursuit of von Spee; and they signalled Cradock on the 16th (signal *No. 6*) that he need no longer keep his cruisers concentrated nor, by implication, have the *Canopus* in support. Simultaneously, and without informing Cradock, the *Defence* was ordered to remain at Malta. For all this the Admiralty had one small excuse, the deceptive north-westerly course steered by von Spee when he left Apia.

But they had no such justification for repeating it a week later when the German ships appeared 1,350 miles further to the *east* off Tahiti, when no fresh action was taken against the possibility of von Spee meeting Cradock who was now sending some of his ships into the Pacific in pursuit of the *Dresden* and, in accordance with the Admiralty's instructions (signal *No. 5*), to stop German trade on the west coast of South America (signal *No. 7*).

It was not, however, too late to retrieve the situation, when the Admiralty learned that the *Scharnhorst*, *Gneisenau* and *Nürnberg* were on their way to Easter Island, if rapid and decisive action had been taken to reinforce Cradock. Instead, they instructed Cradock (signal *No. 10*) to be prepared to meet the German force with the *Canopus*, *Glasgow*, *Monmouth* (or *Good Hope*) and *Otranto*. If he had previously had doubts about the Admiralty's suggestion that his two old armoured cruisers, supported by an even older battleship were a superior force to the *Scharnhorst* and *Gneisenau*, what must have been Cradock's reaction to a suggestion that, augmented by the *Nürnberg*, they could be countered by only one of his armoured cruisers, again supported by the *Canopus*, together with a light cruiser and an armed liner? His reply (signal *No. 11*), in which he added that von Spee's force was likely to comprise two armoured cruisers and *three* light cruisers, is remarkable for its restraint. But he confused matters by not making his intentions clear: whilst he had ordered the *Canopus* to the Falkland Islands 'where I intend to concentrate and avoid division of forces', three of his ships were, apparently, to operate in the Pacific. Nor did his amplifying message of the 11th (signal *No. 12*) do much to assist the Admiralty to understand him.

None the less, Churchill and Battenberg agreed on the 14th that Cradock should concentrate his main force at the Falklands, only the *Glasgow* going round into the Pacific. And they recognised that, pending the arrival of reinforcements, Cradock's squadron might have to limit its object to locating and shadowing the enemy. But the reply to Cradock (signal *No. 13*) did not say this: he was only told that a force under Stoddart was being sent to the east coast and, 'your concentration of *Good Hope*, *Canopus*, *Monmouth*, *Glasgow* and *Otranto* for combined operations [is] concurred in'. Related to Cradock's intention to send the *Glasgow*, *Monmouth* and *Otranto* into the Pacific, together with his subsequent suggestion that a force to meet von Spee was now needed on each coast, this could be taken as authorising him to provide the Pacific force instead of concentrating at the Falkland Islands. Moreover he was left with the impression that his object was still that signalled to him on 14th September, 'to destroy the German cruisers' (signal *No. 5*). He expressed this clearly enough four days later when informing the Admiralty (signal *No. 15*) that the *Canopus*'s speed limited his squadron to 12 knots; 'but shall trust circumstances will enable me to force an action'. In the Admiralty, however, this message was taken to mean that Cradock was acting in accordance with *their* latest wishes, concentrating his force at the Falklands.

They were disillusioned a week later by Cradock's signal *No. 16*. They did not, however, intervene for three reasons: Stoddart's force was assembling on the east coast of South America and could be moved down to the Falklands; by the time the signal reached Whitehall Cradock was already in the Pacific; and they believed he was complying with their instructions to use the *Canopus* in support of his cruisers for what they had decided on 14th October his task should be: 'if not strong enough to attack, he will do his utmost to shadow them, pending the arrival of reinforcements'. That this was far from being Cradock's interpretation might have been clear from his signal *No. 17* in which he not only referred to destroying the enemy's squadron, but informed the Admiralty that the *Canopus* was so useless for this purpose that he intended to employ her escorting his colliers and had ordered the *Defence* to join him in her place. Cradock did not, however, specify that he intended to dispense with the *Canopus*'s support *before* the *Defence* joined him; and he irritated a busy Admiralty by concluding his signal with an obscure reference to his meeting with the *Karlsrühe* on 6th August. These two points explain the Admiralty's reply (signal *No. 18*) to the effect that he already had a sufficient force to engage von Spee (his orders to the *Defence* being cancelled) which chanced to reach him early on the afternoon of 1st November, when he was seeking the *Leipzig*. And it must have confirmed in his mind that he was intended to fight the *Scharnhorst* and *Gneisenau* when he sighted them a couple of hours later, even though he had not been provided with adequate strength to ensure success.

The measure of the Admiralty's responsibility for Coronel is, then, this: initially, whilst appreciating the importance of destroying the two German armoured cruisers, they allowed Allied warships in Far East waters to be employed on other less vital tasks: in mid-September they made a serious error of judgment in deciding that von Spee was going west instead of east so that Cradock's squadron was not reinforced: they came to believe that the *Good Hope* and *Monmouth* supported by the

Canopus, were a squadron of sufficient strength to deal with von Spee; and, perhaps most important of all, their instructions to Cradock were so ineptly worded that the admiral supposed he was intended to seek an action even though his force might be inadequate to gain a victory. Churchill's verdict and his argument in support of it, contained in *The World Crisis*, are thus exposed as being as specious as the British Government's denial of Lord George Germain's responsibility for Burgoyne's surrender at Saratoga in 1777.

Why, then, did the Admiralty make these mistakes? One explanation was aptly expressed by Admiral Wemyss in 1919: the Admiralty needs 'a large and efficient staff organisation. At the commencement of the war this, I am afraid, was lamentably inadequate, and it is only now that, with hard experience to guide us, we have reached a point when it can be truly said that there exists an efficient and admirable Naval Staff.' In the Napoleonic wars the extent to which the Admiralty could operate (as distinct from administering) the fleet was limited to issuing orders and instructions of a general nature to the admirals who commanded Britain's fleets and squadrons. The preparation of these orders was well within the personal capacity of the Lords of the Admiralty Board, aided by an efficient Secretary and a few clerks. A hundred years brought two revolutions: telegraphic communication, first by land line, then by cable, and finally by wireless, gave the Admiralty the power to control the world-wide dispositions of its ships and to direct their employment from day to day; and maritime operations were complicated by technical developments, notably the introduction of steam, and long-range guns, the invention of torpedoes and mines, and the birth of the submarine. These placed the conduct of naval operations beyond the capacity of individuals: admirals needed trained staff officers to cope with the manifold details, to advise them wisely and to implement their decisions with clear and comprehensive orders and instructions.

The British Army had begun to learn this lesson more than 100 years earlier. Before the end of the eighteenth century the Duke of York had inaugurated an embryonic staff college at Sandhurst; the Crimean War had firmly established it at Camberley in 1857. Generals had thus had a century in which to learn how to use adequate staffs. Moreover, after the South African War, the anachronistic office of Commander-in-Chief of the British Army was abolished by the Esher Committee and all responsibility for planning war on land, and its execution, vested in the War Office, with an effective General Staff. The Royal Navy had made no comparable advance. As late as 1893, Tryon, as Commander-in-Chief of the Mediterranean Fleet, could give an order, without a staff to advise him of its folly, that resulted in the sinking of his flagship and his own death. And only in that same decade did the Admiralty acquire a small Naval Staff (of untrained staff officers) inaccurately called the Naval Intelligence Department because its duties included plans for mobilisation. This anachronism was rectified by the report of the Tyrell Committee which in 1909 examined Admiral Sir Charles Beresford's sharp criticisms of the Admiralty, but it did little else. 'How we can be expected to be prepared for war without such a staff is so incomprehensible to me that I am at a loss to understand why Fisher stands out against it', wrote Richmond. Though he was a member of the Esher Committee that gave the Army a General Staff, it was as repugnant to Fisher to delegate power to others, as it was that comparatively junior officers should voice their opinions on the conduct of war. He preferred to do his own thinking: 'a Naval War Staff at the Admiralty is a very excellent organisation for cutting out and arranging foreign newspaper clippings', although in 1902, before becoming First Sea Lord he had written a paper 'On the Increasing Necessity for a General Staff for the Navy to meet War Requirements'.

Fisher, and his successor, Admiral of the Fleet Sir Arthur Wilson, believed that war plans should be prepared by the First Sea Lord alone and divulged to no one. Fortunately the Agadir crisis occurred in 1911; when Wilson failed to sustain his objections to disclosing his plans to the Cabinet, the Admiralty's and the War Office's plans for war were discovered to be so fundamentally different that the Secretary of State for War, Haldane, intimated to the Prime Minister that he could not continue to be responsible for the War Office unless a Board of Admiralty was called into being which would work in full harmony with the War Office, and would begin the organisation of a proper Naval War Staff. This had four results: the dynamic Churchill was appointed First Lord to put the Admiralty's house in order; Wilson, because he categorically refused to create a Naval War Staff, was replaced, first by Admiral Bridgeman, then, in March 1913, by Battenberg; a Naval War Staff was established at the beginning of 1912; and a staff course was grafted on to the War College in Portsmouth Dockyard to train officers to serve it. The War College had been opened in 1907 by Fisher to remedy senior naval officers' preoccupation with material developments, though this was too late to rectify the defect pungently expressed by Churchill: 'We had more captains of ships than captains of war'. But these changes could not, in the short space of three years turn the Admiralty into the efficient machine needed for the effective conduct of operations in a twentieth century world war: Such a task requires a generation.

> The War Staff [Richmond noted in his diary] was . . . a body which never was nor ever could be a war staff as it was deficient in all the characteristics that are needed for staff work. . . . The whole of the work passes through the Chief of Staff. There is no decentralisation, and his mind has to grapple with every problem that arises, even in its details. . . . The result of this fear to decentralise is that the First Sea Lord and Chief of Staff are [so] overworked that they cannot foresee and provide in advance, that they cannot consider suggestions brought to them and, finally, that a mass of officers is assembled under the Admiralty roof many of whom are wholly unfit for their duties.

This in large part explains the Admiralty's failings which led to Coronel.

Seriously defective though the machine was, it cannot absolve from responsibility those who were at the controls at the time. Pre-eminent, by virtue of office, was Churchill. For much of the eighteenth century and until after Trafalgar, the First Lord of the Admiralty was both a naval officer and in Parliament. Men like Anson, Hawke, Howe, St Vincent and Barham were as well qualified to conduct the affairs of the Navy in war as they were to answer for it to the nation. They combined, in effect, the offices of First Lord and First Sea Lord: before the nineteenth century the naval or professional lords were no more than their assistants (though Barham went so far as making the First the equivalent of Chief of Staff, thereby establishing the pre-eminent position which he has since occupied). The nineteenth-century ban on naval officers standing for Parliament put an end to this practice: the First Lord became a political figure; the direct control of the Navy passed into the hands of the First Naval Lord. But the very fact that Churchill had been sent to the Admiralty because Wilson had shown himself unwilling to co-operate with the War Office in planning for the expected war, and unwilling to institute the necessary reforms, was more than enough for a man of his calibre to concern himself directly with naval operations to a much greater degree than any other politician of his time. He was not leaving their conduct to the First Sea Lord.

Much that Churchill did in this sphere is not open to criticism; he alone among British statesmen of the First World War understood the advantage to Britain of a maritime strategy, notably his concept of forcing the Dardanelles which, if it had not been starved of the necessary ships and men, including competent commanders, by those who had no eyes except for the North Sea and the Western Front, if it had not been such a deplorable story of vacillation, delay and divided counsels among the Allied high commands, could so easily have succeeded, and ended the war earlier than 1918. But his methods of doing business, the constant bombardment of memoranda and minutes on every conceivable subject, the consultation with others on matters entirely within the province of the First Sea Lord, were bound to cause friction—though it was not until 1915 that he developed the objectionable habit of sending operational signals to naval authorities 'from First Lord' instead of 'from Admiralty', or of sending them 'from Admiralty' marked 'First Sea Lord to see *after* despatch'. He was, moreover, only 40 years old; he could not always gain the support of his older colleagues in the Cabinet, though Hankey has recorded that 'we owed a good deal in those early days to the courage and inspiration of Winston Churchill who, undaunted by difficulties and losses, set an infectious example to those of his colleagues who had given less thought than he, if indeed any thought at all, to war problems. He may have been rash at times, but he was a tower of strength and I hope his fellow countrymen will never forget it, in spite of the tremendous addition he has since made to his claims to an outstanding place in history.' Nor could he confine his zest for war to matters which were the Admiralty's sphere of responsibility: by his direction the Navy undertook the defence of London against zeppelin attack and the Admiralty designed the first tanks ('land ships') for the Army. More relevant, he was not content with sending a naval brigade to defend Antwerp in October and paying the place a visit at a most critical time: he must suggest that he should assume personal command. Though the Cabinet would not approve this, he was absent from the Admiralty for the best part of a week at a critical time so far as Coronel is concerned. For this and kindred reasons the attention which he gave to von Spee's approach to South America and the measures needed to meet his squadron was spasmodic. So to Churchill belongs a considerable measure of personal responsibility for the disaster—though the historian of today must add that it was out of the experience which this unique man acquired in 1914 and the following years that his genius for conducting war developed into the wondrous flower that gained for Britain, by a proper use of maritime strategy, a second and greater victory over German aggression in 1939–45.

The man at the Admiralty who, with any other First Lord, would have born direct responsibility for Coronel was, in Fisher's words:

'Prince Louis of Battenberg [who is] the very ablest admiral after Sir Arthur Wilson that we possess both afloat and ashore'—and in Churchill's: 'Prince Louis was a child of the Royal Navy . . . bred to the sea. . . . All his interest was centred in the British Fleet. . . . He had spent an exceptionally large proportion of his forty years' service afloat. . . . He had a far wider knowledge of war by land and sea . . . than most of the other admirals I have known. He was a thoroughly trained and accomplished staff officer, with a gift of clear and lucid statement and (of) thoroughness and patient industry.' No responsible person has denied those tributes: no naval officer of Battenberg's time doubted that he was the man who should be at the Admiralty's helm in war. Even Captain Richmond, who was so often censorious, wrote: 'Battenberg is . . . worth a hundred of the others.' As First Sea Lord he had to deal with a dozen crises at sea at the same time and he had to face the threat of invasion, then believed to be serious. The dangers in the outer seas, such as von Spee's squadron and the *Emden*, occupied second place in his mind to the High Seas Fleet in home waters. The stupendous task of mastering the details of ever-changing situations, many of great complexity, without the help of an effective War Staff, was too much for any individual who bore such an appalling weight of responsibility. But Battenberg also laboured under two other handicaps; he had to expend much of the time and energy which he should have devoted to the naval war to contending with his forceful political master—and he was no Alanbrooke; and throughout October his mind was increasingly distracted by circumstances so cruel that he would have been superhuman if his vigour and imagination had not been impaired. This culminated on the 28th in a letter to Churchill: 'I have lately been driven to the painful conclusion that at this juncture my birth and parentage have the effect of impairing in some respects my usefulness in the Board of Admiralty. In these circumstances I feel it my duty . . . to resign the office of First Sea Lord.'

The climate of opinion was such that the First Lord saw no alternative to accepting Battenberg's offer in a letter in which he rightly referred to 'the burden of responsibility you have borne thus far with such honour and success'. But well might *The Times* leader writer say: '[Prince Louis's] action is unquestionably the result of a campaign of suggestion—part of it honest if ill-timed, part of it monstrously unjust —against his remaining head of the Navy. . . . He has also been attacked by hardly less open gossip and innuendo for his German birth, and it is upon this ground that his resignation is based. Of [this] charge it is difficult to write with patience. . . .' Lord Selborne, who had himself been a distinguished First Lord, wrote: 'That anyone should have been found to insinuate suspicions against him is nothing less than a national humiliation'; and a Labour spokesman, Mr J. H. Thomas, expressed the same sentiments. This shameful business cannot deny Battenberg's major responsibility for the Admiralty's part in Coronel, but its distraction, together with the extent to which he was required to work in double harness with such a man as Churchill, go a long way towards excusing him for it.

One cannot omit the name of Admiral Sir Henry Jackson, who had been Chief of the Naval War Staff until June, 1914. Appointed special adviser on overseas operations and President of the special sub-committee of the Committee of Imperial Defence established to deal with Germany's colonies overseas, he encouraged the Australian and New Zealand attacks on New Guinea and Samoa in August, 1914, which required Patey's squadron to protect these expeditions when it might have been deployed against von Spee's armoured cruisers before they left the western Pacific. His share of the Admiralty's responsibility for Coronel is, perhaps, comparable with that of Rear-Admiral Leveson, Director of the Operations Division of the Naval War Staff. Too often he rejected his subordinates' appreciations of the threat presented by von Spee and the need for an adequate force on the west coast of South America to meet it—though his task cannot have been an easy one when his assistant director was that 'turbulent priest' among naval officers, albeit a brilliant and unorthodox one, Captain Richmond. As often, when he accepted such an appreciation, he failed to press it on his superiors, however convincing the arguments.

> He said he had done his best about the *Scharnhorst* and *Gneisenau*, when I [Richmond] reproached him for not forcing out reinforcements. What he did I don't know. But having seen him in Sturdee's room sometimes when discussions were in progress on which I more or less knew his views, he appeared to me to suppress them very effectively in the face of his superior. I like him immensely. But I can't help feeling there's a weak point behind all that appearance of strength.

Leveson, be it added, did not remain at the Admiralty for very long after Fisher replaced Battenberg, because he had been flag captain to Admiral Sir William May, another officer whom the new First Sea Lord detested.

Oliver cannot be wholly ignored, but as Naval Secretary his duty was no greater than to feed the First Lord with the Naval War Staff's views. He is not, for example, to be blamed for the disastrously wrong appreciation which he summed up for Churchill on 29th October in the minute quoted on page 93.

There remains Leveson's immediate superior, Sturdee, Battenberg's principal adviser and deputy. He had the advantage of enjoying Battenberg's confidence—the First Sea Lord had specifically nominated him for appointment as Chief of Staff; but he suffered the handicap of having assumed control of the newly-fledged Naval War Staff less than three months before it was plunged into conducting a world-wide war. And he was by nature and experience ill-fitted for the task. His keen analytical brain lacked the flexibility of mind and incisive ability for quick decisions required of the head of an operational staff in war. He was among those who could not appreciate the serious threat presented by U-boats; he did not see that large cruisers (the *Aboukir*, *Cressy* and *Hogue*) on a slow patrol in the southern part of the North Sea were sitting ducks for this new type of warfare. He had been chief of staff to Beresford in the Mediterranean, but that appointment was concerned more with the administration of the fleet than operations. Beatty's comment to his flag captain at Jutland: 'There is something wrong with our bloody ships today, Chatfield' is famous. Less well known, but more important, is that he added: 'And there is something wrong with our system.' He might mean it of the Grand Fleet's rigid tactics; but it was as true of admirals' inability to use their staffs. And Sturdee was a victim of this 'system'; he had not been brought up to delegate either responsibility or action. 'No wave of the wand can create those habits of mind in seniors on which the efficiency and even the reality of a staff depends.' He could not direct the War Staff to prepare an appreciation; he must do one himself. He could not authorise a signal to be drafted; he must laboriously write it in his own hand. As one result, he was monstrously overwhelmed with work so that urgent action was often delayed. 'Oliver [noted Richmond] showed me a telegram today which he had written for dispatch on 4th October, but which was not sent until the 8th, having been held up by the C.O.S.' Nor could he function as an effective deputy for the First Sea Lord when the circumstances which led to his resignation rendered Battenberg no longer fully competent to make the decisions which were properly his, when the Naval War Staff was not such an efficient machine that it could maintain its momentum without the First Sea Lord's inspired direction. John Buchan says of one of his fictional characters: 'No man ever saw him rattled or hustled': one could say as much of Sturdee. The latter characteristic mitigated against him as Chief of Staff—but the former was soon to gain him a place in history's hall of fame. Sturdee personified the deficiencies of the Naval War Staff which only a blazing genius could have surmounted, and his greatest admirers would hesitate to make any such claim. Those who, like Richmond, saw in him the real 'villain of the piece' conveniently forgot Fisher's failure to provide the Admiralty with a War Staff during his first period as First Sea Lord.

The action taken by the Admiralty on 3rd November supports these criticisms of individuals. Forced to find a new First Sea Lord at a critical stage of the war at sea, Churchill brought Fisher back to office. He might now be 74, but much of his genius remained. 'Everything began to move. Inertia disappeared. The huge machine creaked and groaned; but it began to turn out work at an increased rate.' But he could not be expected to absorb all the details of a world-wide war at sea immediately, and consider whether every action taken to counter German moves was adequate. On 30th October Churchill took him to the War Room and 'went over with him on the great map the positions and tasks of every vessel in our immense organisation. It took more than two hours. The critical point was clearly in South American waters. Speaking of Cradock's position, I said: "You don't suppose he would try to fight them without the *Canopus*?" He did not give any decided reply.' But when the signal from Valparaiso reached Whitehall reporting von Spee's arrival off the coast of Chile, Fisher realised at once the inadequacy of Cradock's force and the danger inherent in his intentions. It was not his fault that signal *No. 19*, in whose wording the new directing hand is clear, went out too late.

One final point before we have done with Coronel: only Churchill went so far as to claim that Whitehall held *no* responsibility for the disaster. When Cradock's memorial was unveiled in York Minster in 1916, a new First Lord, Arthur Balfour, included these words in a just tribute to the dead admiral:

> Why, then, you will ask me, did he attack—deliberately, designedly, intentionally—a force which he could not have reasonably hoped either to destroy or put to flight? I think a satisfactory explanation can be given. Remember what the circumstances of the German squadron were. They were not like those of the German High Seas Fleet . . . close to their own ports, capable of taking in a damaged ship to their own dockyards, and their own protected bases. The German admiral in the Pacific was very differently situated. He was far from any port where he could have refitted. No friendly bases were open to him. If, therefore,

he suffered damage, even though in suffering damage he apparently inflicted greater damage than he received, yet his power, great for evil while he remained untouched, might suddenly . . . be utterly destroyed. He would be a great peril as long as his squadron remained efficient, and [if] Admiral Cradock . . . judged that his squadron, that he himself and those under him, were well sacrificed if they destroyed the power of this hostile fleet, then I say that there is no man, be he sailor or be he civilian, but would say that such a judgment showed not only the highest courage, but the greatest courage of unselfishness; and that Admiral Cradock, by absolute neglect of personal interest and personal ambitions, had shown a wise judgment in the interests of his country. If I am right there never was a nobler act.

We shall never know the thoughts of Admiral Cradock when it became evident that, out-gunned and out-ranged, success was an impossibility. He must have realised that his hopes were dashed for ever to the ground, that his plan had failed. His body is separated from us by half the world, and he and his gallant comrades lie far from the pleasant homes of England. Yet they have their reward, and we are surely right in saying that theirs is an immortal place in the great role of naval heroes.

Part two

THE FALKLANDS

4

Thirty-six Days

'I am quite homeless. I cannot reach Germany; we possess
no other secure harbour; I must plough the seas of the world
doing as much mischief as I can, till my ammunition is exhausted, or till a foe far superior in power succeeds in
catching me.'

Von Spee at Valparaiso

ON 3rd November, two days after Coronel, the *Scharnhorst*, *Gneisenau*
and *Nürnberg* anchored in Valparaiso Roads. Since International Law
prohibited more than three belligerent warships visiting a neutral port
at the same time, the *Leipzig* and *Dresden* had been detached and sent
to Mas a Fuera, which was so sparsely inhabited that von Spee could
afford to ignore its Chilean ownership. The same law allowed von Spee
just 24 hours to signal news of his victory to Berlin; to ensure that the
Good Hope, of whose fate he was uncertain, would be interned if she
put into a Chilean port for repairs; to gain intelligence of Allied naval
dispositions; and to assess his prospects of keeping his squadron
supplied with coal, before deciding his next move. The British minister
protested in vain against the visit.

The 32 German merchant ships anchored in Valparaiso were, for
von Spee, 'an exhilarating sight but, alas, all of them confined to the
harbour by the sea power of England'. And the reception he and his
crews received from the local populace was heart-warming. 'When I
landed there were crowds at the landing stage. Cameras clicked every-
where and here and there small groups raised cheers.' But though the
officers and men from the *Scharnhorst* and *Gneisenau* enjoyed their first
visit to a city for more than three months, this was not their admiral's
mood after he had seen the German minister. Von Erckerdt expected to
be able to continue sending coal to the squadron despite the British
minister's strenuous efforts to prevent ships sailing with supplies from

Chilean ports, but he had news of Japanese reinforcements heading for North American waters, and he handed von Spee a telegram from Berlin:

> Lines of rendezvous [with German colliers] in the Atlantic are all compromised, all trade routes being strongly patrolled. In the Atlantic cruiser warfare can only be carried on by ships operating in groups. *Karlsrühe* and *Kronprinz Wilhelm* have orders to combine. It is intended to concentrate all forces and order them to break through for home in groups.

'To break through for home', when the way was barred by the whole might of the Grand Fleet! 'The Germans, of course, wanted to celebrate but I positively refused. I was forced, however, to spend one and a half hours at their club', when a civilian proposed the toast: 'Damnation to the British Navy!' Von Spee's response cut the cheerful atmosphere with the chill of the surgeon's knife. 'I drink', he said, 'to the memory of a gallant and honourable foe.'

Next morning von Erckerdt gave him a further signal from Berlin: 'You are advised to try and break through with all your ships and return home.' Yesterday's message had been intended for all Germany's marauding cruisers; this was addressed to von Spee. It had, however, been dispatched as soon as Berlin knew that the squadron had arrived off the Chilean coast, before they had knews of Coronel. And it was not a positive order: 'You are advised . . .' was all it said. But what other course was open to the German admiral? His eastward voyage across the Pacific had shown that an attempt to retrace his steps would not be worth the risk of running into Patey's powerful squadron. A move north was barred by the Japanese whose strength indicated that it would be unwise to head for the Panama Canal. He might remain for a while off the west coast of South America, strangling Allied maritime trade. But since the time must come when his ships would need refitting, he had no ultimate alternative to proceeding round the Horn into the Atlantic.

Nonetheless, von Spee had not reached a decision when his ships sailed from Valparaiso to rejoin the *Dresden* and *Leipzig* at Mas a Fuera. He had, however, met an old acquaintance, a retired German naval doctor, and to him confided the words which head this chapter. And just as he was about to reboard his flagship, a lady handed him a bouquet of arum lilies: 'Thank you,' said von Spee, 'they will do very nicely for my grave.' These incidents, and all else that we know of the

German admiral's visit to the Chilean port, suggest that the strain of his exceptionally difficult command was beginning to tell on him; that with the prospects of even greater difficulties ahead, he was no longer capable of the incisive thought essential for success. For it must have been clear that the British would react to the news of Coronel by dispatching strong reinforcements to hunt him down: the sooner the German squadron entered the South Atlantic the better would be its chances. Yet, although von Spee decided to round the Horn during his stay at Mas a Fuera, he evinced no haste to do so. In contrast to his voyage across the Pacific, when he cruised slowly to save coal but, except towards the end, spent little time in harbour, he now remained at anchor for some 10 days whilst he sent the *Dresden* and *Leipzig* to Valparaiso to give the lie to a strong rumour that these two ships had been sunk at Coronel, though their visit from 13th to 14th November also told the British Admiralty that the German squadron was still in the area. It was not until 15th November that the *Scharnhorst*, *Gneisenau* and *Nürnberg*, accompanied by the supply ships *Baden* and *Santa Isabel*, sailed south, leaving the *Prinz Eitel Friedrich* to make wireless transmission to mislead the Japanese squadron into supposing the German force to be still there.

When the *Dresden* and *Leipzig* rejoined at sea on the 18th, they brought von Spee a letter from Berlin:

> We recommend you to carry on cruiser warfare as rigorously as the Prize Law permits. . . . Cruiser warfare in the Pacific offers few prospects of success. In view of the strict patrolling of the main trade routes in the Atlantic, cruiser warfare will only be possible for ships operating in groups strong enough to meet the enemy if he interferes. On the other hand the coaling of ships in groups will become more and more difficult. . . . It is therefore left to your discretion to break off cruiser warfare as soon as you think it advisable and to make your way home with all the forces you can concentrate. . . . It seems possible that you may succeed . . . if your careful preparations are accompanied by good luck. . . . It may be necessary to secure the co-operation of the High Seas Fleet in breaking through the enemy's patrol lines in the North Sea; you should therefore notify your intentions in good time. . . .

Though the letter was dated 10th October these instructions agreed with the two signals the German admiral had already received. But the subsequent paragraphs, which detailed Allied naval dispositions in the North Sea and Atlantic, the attitude of the various neutral countries bordering this ocean, and the situation in Germany's African colonies were of limited value, being nearly a month old ('Togo is entirely in the enemy's hands. . . . As for the Cameroons, the British have captured Duala . . . [and their] forces have been landed in German South-West Africa'), though one sentence—'The *Invincible*, *Inflexible* and *Indomitable* have probably been withdrawn from the Mediterranean'—had a fateful significance despite its inaccuracies.

Six days later, on 21st November, the German squadron found a safe anchorage in St Quentin Bay. Here a signal brought news that the Kaiser had bestowed Iron Crosses First and Second Class on von Spee, and had allocated 300 Iron Crosses Second Class to his officers and men. And with this encouragement the admiral was content to stay at St Quentin until the 26th, making unhurried preparations for the next leg of his voyage. His cruisers filled their bunkers from three colliers that had slipped out of Chilean ports without obtaining clearance for their cargoes; they also piled their decks with coal. And when the squadron sailed again nearly four weeks after Coronel, it had three supply ships in company, the *Baden*, the *Santa Isabel* and the *Seydlitz*. In all they had enough coal to carry them well up the east coast of South America; for as von Spee wrote to his wife: 'How our future activities will develop lies in God's hand, and though I naturally have my plans, yet the possible contingencies are so many that I must be prepared for everything. What would be most unpleasant, is the cutting off of the coal supply, and this is very doubtful', a sentence prompted by a signal he had received from Buenos Aires 'that coal cannot be sent in steamers from Argentine and Brazilian ports, coal export being prohibited.' He hoped, nonetheless, to find colliers from Montevideo awaiting him at Port Santa Elena on 5th December.

In taking so long to reach the Horn von Spee made an error of judgment as vital to his future as any made by Cradock: he was yet to make another. Before, however, recording this, it should be noted that Berlin was as much responsible for the Falkland Islands disaster as Whitehall for Cradock's death. When von Spee's telegram announcing his victory on 1st November reached Berlin, Tirpitz, knowing only that Stoddart had an appreciable force on the east coast of South America,

> proposed to put him [von Spee] free from the east coast to run up the centre of the Atlantic. I intended . . . to draw Count Spee's attention to his shortage of ammunition, and that we did not expect any further activities of him and that the main part of his task now was to make his way homewards. . . . The prestige of Coronel would have been maintained. As Count Spee was not informed of the general position of the

19   *S.M.S.* Scharnhorst *embarking stores in* Valparaiso Roads *after Coronel*

20　*Von Spee* (right) *with the German Minister, von Erckerdt,*
at Valparaiso after Coronel

21　*The German cruisers* Scharnhorst (right) *and* Gneisenau *leaving Valparaiso*

war such instructions seemed desirable, but the Chief of Naval Staff, Admiral von Pohl, thought it unwise to encroach on the freedom of action of the Count, whom he thought would be better informed of the strength of the English force than we were.

Tirpitz was right in his appreciation that von Spee had travelled so far from his peace-time station that he could not now know enough to make sound plans, but he could not over-rule von Pohl's decision to cling to the German principle of leaving the matter to the man on the spot. Not until the middle of November did the Chief of Naval Staff signal von Spee: 'What are your plans? How much ammunition have you?' 'The Cruiser Squadron intends to break through for home', was the laconic reply, to which was added the information that the two armoured cruisers had approximately half their ammunition remaining and the light cruisers rather more.

Before leaving St Quentin, von Spee also learned that the German naval agent in San Francisco had asked Berlin to send a battle-cruiser into the North Atlantic to support the squadron's return. Fortunately for his already pessimistic frame of mind, observing what had been said in the letter from Berlin about the possibility of co-operation by the High Seas Fleet, the admiral does not appear to have received the discouraging answer, a testament to the reality of the Grand Fleet's North Sea blockade: 'Impossible to despatch a large cruiser from home to the North Atlantic.' The same German agent seems to have been the only man to urge on von Spee the need for haste, signalling him on 11th November: 'If the Cruiser Squadron decides to return home it appears advisable for it to leave immediately. In my opinion it is dangerously situated.' Von Spee might have agreed with this appreciation on 7th November when he received intelligence that the *Defence, Cornwall, Carnarvon, Bristol, Glasgow* and *Canopus* were concentrated at the Falkland Islands. But British wireless activity, which had been considerable, then ceased, suggesting that the force had left for some other destination. And this seemed to be confirmed by subsequent intelligence from Montevideo to the effect that the British ships had been ordered to South Africa to assist in dealing with the Boer revolt.

How far was this true? Aboard the *Canopus* 'for the next forty-eight hours [after Coronel] it was a very anxious time', wrote one of her officers. 'We could only do 14–15 knots [*see note on p. 181*] and the *Scharnhorst* and *Gneisenau* can do 22 [*sic*], so if they had followed us we might have been caught easily. We came down through all the narrow channels amongst the islands off the Chilean coast and safely reached the Magellan Straits. We expected to meet [the enemy] at the entrance and were all prepared, but no, they were not there. . . . Soon after we heard from the *Glasgow*' which had run south at 20 knots, where, one of her officers remembers, 'everything [was] very uncomfortable and everybody very silent and depressed. Carpenters hard at work shoring up all round the damage aft. Captain's cabin still unapproachable for cordite fumes. Great seas over forecastle all day.' On 4th November there was an 'exciting minute when [the *Glasgow*] made entrance to Magellan Straits at 1000 as enemy could possibly have intercepted us. Fine cold weather. Passed Punta Arenas during the night.' On the 6th the two ships met in Lomas Bay and heard that the *Otranto* was safely on her own way round the Horn; and Luce was at last able to signal the Admiralty, through the Falkland Islands, a brief report on Coronel.

This was not, however, the first news of the defeat to reach London; a substantial account had arrived from the British consul-general early on the 4th, gleaned from the German ships' visit to Valparaiso. Since Hipper's battle-cruisers had bombarded Yarmouth without hindrance by British forces only the day before, it was not an auspicious moment. (Not until three months later did the Admiralty have the satisfaction of learning that on this same day the elusive *Karlsrühe* was sunk off Trinidad by an internal explosion due to unstable cordite.) Indeed, the Admiralty doubted the accuracy of the report because it made no mention of the *Canopus*: they could not believe that Cradock had engaged von Spee without the old battleship's support. *The Times* said: 'If the report be true there is only one explanation: Admiral Cradock fell into a trap.' But when the Admiralty was able to publish a communiqué based on Luce's signal, criticism by a shocked press and public mounted, not of Cradock, but of the Admiralty. 'It is my duty', said Lord Selborne in Parliament on the 12th, 'to ask how it possibly came about that such a squadron as that which has been in large part destroyed could have been chosen to defend our flag in the Pacific against such a squadron of cruisers as Germany sent forward. . . . For the purpose of defeating the German squadron the addition of the *Canopus* was obviously futile.' And Bonar Law said as much in the House of Commons.

Long before this, however, before the receipt of Luce's signal, the First Lord and the First Sea Lord, 'a genius without doubt' and 'a veritable dynamo', as they described each other, had acted in concert to avenge the first defeat the Royal Navy had suffered for more than 100 years. Fisher's drive was already making the Admiralty quiver like one of his great ships at its highest speed. On 4th November an urgent signal went to Stoddart:

> . . . *Carnarvon*, *Cornwall* should join *Defence* off Montevideo. *Canopus*, *Glasgow*, *Otranto* have been ordered, if possible, to join you there. *Kent* from Sierra Leone has also been ordered to join your flag via Abrolhos. . . . Enemy will most likely come on to the Rio trade route. Reinforcements will meet you shortly from England.

Another went to the Governor of the Falkland Islands:

> German cruiser raid may take place. All Admiralty colliers should be concealed in unfrequented harbours. Be ready to destroy supplies useful to enemy and hide codes effectively on ships being sighted.

A third was far more important; Churchill, remembering Battenberg's and Sturdee's earlier suggestions, proposed sending a battle-cruiser to reinforce Stoddart. 'But I found Lord Fisher in bolder mood. He would take two of these powerful ships', each, like Patey's *Australia*, armed with eight 12-inch guns and with a speed of 25 knots. So the dramatic signal went out to the C.-in-C. Grand Fleet:

> Order *Invincible* and *Inflexible* to fill up with coal at once and proceed to Berehaven with all dispatch. They are urgently needed for foreign service. Admiral and flag captain *Invincible* to transfer to *New Zealand*. *Tiger* ordered to join you with all dispatch.

'Sir John Jellicoe rose to the occasion and parted with his two battle-cruisers without a word', when a personal signal from the First Lord explained the service for which they were required, although he had lost the battleship *Audacious* on a mine only a week before. But he was far from happy about his margin of superiority over the High Seas Fleet when, on 10th November, the Admiralty ordered him to send the *Princess Royal* to North America to guard against the possibility of von Spee coming through the Panama Canal and attempting to assist German liners which could be converted into armed merchant cruisers to break out from their New York sanctuary. But Churchill and Fisher, noting that, in addition to the *Tiger*, the new battleships *Benbow*, *Emperor of India* and *Queen Elizabeth* were practically ready, accepted the risk. To these two men therefore goes chief credit for a strategic move which was to prove as decisive as any in our history (though Richmond, whose earlier advice on the need for strong measures to deal with von

Spee had been rejected, characteristically criticised it in his diary: 'The inevitable result of our initial mistake is now making itself felt. Through not having sent *Defence* and two others in time . . . now follows over-doing it). But it might have been otherwise if these two giants had not realised also the need for *swift* action. After arriving at Devonport (instead of Berehaven, to enable the admiral chosen to command them to join without delay), the Admiral Superintendent, who had little knowledge of the service for which the ships were required, signalled that the earliest date by which the *Invincible* and *Inflexible* could be ready to sail again (after coaling, remedying defects, and embarking three months' supply of stores, together with stores for other ships in South American waters, plus ammunition to fill the *Glasgow*'s depleted magazines) was 13th November. On hearing this, Churchill immediately expressed 'great discontent with the dockyard delays and asked: "Shall I give him a prog?" or words to that effect. Fisher took up the signal. As soon as he saw it he exclaimed: "Friday the thirteenth. What a day to choose!" I then wrote and signed the following order which was the direct cause of the battle of the Falklands:

> *Admiralty to C.-in-C. Devonport.* Ships are to sail on Wednesday 11th. They are needed for war service and dockyard arrangements must be made to conform. If necessary dockyard men should be sent away in the ships. You are held responsible for the speedy dispatch of these ships in a thoroughly efficient condition. Acknowledge. *W.S.C.*

They sailed accordingly and in the nick of time.'

Rear-Admiral Sir Archibald Moore had had to transfer from the *Invincible* to the *New Zealand* because he was too junior for the responsibilities Fisher proposed to give to the new appointment of C.-in-C. South Atlantic and South Pacific Station. What other flag officer with the requisite seniority and qualifications was immediately available for an important sea command? On returning to the Admiralty, Fisher had made it clear that he would not tolerate Sturdee as Chief of Staff. When Sturdee had been appointed chief of staff to Beresford in the Mediterranean nearly a decade before, Fisher had wanted him, 'to keep an eye on Charlie as he was inclined to be rash and rather wild on Service matters', Sturdee later noted. 'He asked me to write to him privately about my Chief. This request I never complied with; such a disloyal act was so obvious it did not require a second thought.' But Sturdee's proper loyalty to his commander-in-chief could not save him from becoming anathema to Fisher when, in the years immediately

Cypher A

Admiralty to Vice Admiral Devonport.

Inflexible & Invincible

Ships are to sail Wednesday 11th. They are needed for war service and dockyard arrangements must be made to conform. If necessary dockyard men should be sent away in the ships to return as opportunity may offer. You are held responsible for the speedy despatch of these ships in a thoroughly efficient condition.

COPIED.

1 L Acknowledge
1 SL
DYB
DC for DUD
6 copies

Sent 12.5 a.m. 10/11

22 *A facsimile of the signal quoted opposite in Churchill's own hand: evidence of his genius for war and of the way in which, as political head of the Admiralty, he usurped the functions of the First Sea Lord* preceding the war, Beresford waged a long and bitter public feud against him. Explaining this to Sturdee, Churchill, who had no reason to share Fisher's anathema, suggested that he should relieve Jerram, with his responsibilities extended to overall command of the Indian and Pacific Oceans, including the Australian area, since the operations against the *Emden* had shown the weakness of having three separate commands in that half of the world. But Sturdee rejected the offer because it involved headquarters ashore; to him the only adequate alternative to his present appointment was a sea command. Until that should become available, he was willing to serve as Chief of Staff under Fisher, despite the new First Sea Lord's intense dislike for him; he had no intention of resigning.

There the matter rested until the news of Coronel reached the Admiralty. On the morning of 4th November Fisher came to Sturdee's room and told him that, *on his own responsibility*, he had decided to send two battle-cruisers to the South Atlantic. Sturdee, perhaps not very tactfully, pointed out that he had suggested such a move before Coronel, but that the idea had been turned down.* Fisher flushed with anger and immediately left the room to tell Churchill that he would not tolerate that 'd—d fool as Chief of Staff at the Admiralty' one day longer. The First Lord had to think quickly: he could not dismiss Sturdee without the unjust imputation that he was to blame for Coronel†; by the afternoon he had persuaded Fisher—and very few men could have done as much with that volcanic giant—to agree to him writing Sturdee the following letter:

> As I indicated to you last week the new constitution of the Board of Admiralty renders desirable a rearrangement of the Staff. The destruction of the German squadron concentrated on the west coast of South America is an object of high and immediate importance and I propose

* Immediately the news of the Falkland action was received, one of Sturdee's colleagues at the Admiralty wrote in a congratulatory letter: 'I have stated my opinion very strongly on the subject to (those here) who had been told that the dispatch of this squadron was a new move, the result of the advent of Fisher. I pointed out that you had arranged for a very similar squadron to be sent to South America directly we knew the Germans were crossing the Pacific, but that you had been overruled.'

† Even so, this accusation was made, and not only by the censorious Richmond. Beresford wrote: 'There was an attempt to throw blame on him for loss of the *Good Hope* and *Monmouth*, I do not think that cowardly action will occur again after the remarks made by me in the House (of Lords) on the matter . . .' though this well-meant defence was not likely to improve Fisher's opinion of Sturdee.

to entrust this duty to you. . . . This is one of the most important and attractive duties which is open to a British flag officer at the present time. Let me thank you for the work you have done as Chief of Staff in the opening, and for the Navy the most critical, months of the war.

Sturdee accepted this offer without hesitation: hurriedly turning over to Oliver, who was appointed Chief of Staff in his stead, he hoisted his flag in the *Invincible* on 9th November.

Disregarding the circumstances which brought it about, was Churchill justified in selecting Sturdee for such an important command? Born in 1859, he had entered the *Britannia* at the age of 12, passing first out of the training ship, and all his examinations for lieutenant with great distinction. He saw active service in the 1882 operations at Alexandria, then made his mark as a torpedo specialist on the technical staff of the *Vernon* and in command of torpedo boats. As a commander he served four years at the Admiralty before going to the *Porpoise* in Australia; and whilst there he was in command of the British force in Samoa where there was trouble between Germany and the United States in 1899, when his delicate handling of a tricky international situation gained him the C.M.G. and promotion to captain. A period as Assistant Director of Naval Intelligence preceded active command of several cruisers in home waters where he caught Beresford's eye. He was thus marked out for promotion to flag rank in 1910, at the age of 51, when he became Rear-Admiral First Battle Squadron, then senior cruiser admiral in the Home Fleet. By this time Jellicoe knew him as 'an officer who had made a special study of tactics', and when war came he had the reputation, as Churchill noted, of being 'a sea officer of keen intelligence and great practical ability—a man who could handle and fight his ship and his squadron with the utmost skill and resolution'.

There was, therefore, no doubting Sturdee's professional qualifications. It is not so easy to portray the man who was physically on the small side. The bronze bust in the Royal United Service Museum shows his features better than any photograph, especially his impressive Roman nose and pronounced lower jaw, though the eyes are set too close beneath heavy brows to allow the adjective handsome to be readily applied. But because he lacked the extrovert personality which made Cradock so well liked, contemporary word pictures of his personality are hard to come by. Sir Vincent Baddeley wrote: 'He was a really able naval officer and an indefatigable student of his profession, who made his way to the highest rank entirely by his own merits, hard work and devotion to the Service.' However true, this suggests a cold personality; but one of the *Invincible*'s officers recalls that, though he shunned visits to his flagship's wardroom, he liked a game of bridge in his cabin; and an American war correspondent wrote in *The Times*: 'Along with the peculiar charm and alertness which we associate with sailors . . . he has the quality of the scholar, with a suspicion of merriness in his eye. . . . [He] is so gentle-mannered.' He was certainly human as well as possessing a strong mind of his own, for he married as a young lieutenant of 23 in an era when it was tantamount to professional suicide for a naval officer to take a wife before he reached the rank of commander. And if, sometimes, he seemed aloof of manner, he did not lack one quality vital to the successful admiral, the ability to speak to his men in terms they understood. There are more who remember him for the stirring address he gave the ship's company of the *Invincible* in the presence of Father Neptune on the day the battle-cruisers crossed the Line than recall his lectures to distinguished audiences at the Royal United Service Institution by whom he was twice awarded their gold medal. 'He is a great improvement on the last man [Moore], he is a real admiral [who] doesn't seem to lose his head or get excited', wrote one of the *Invincible*'s officers, a description which highlights the characteristic which was to play so large a part in his pursuit of von Spee.

The *Invincible*, Captain P. T. H. Beamish, and the *Inflexible*, Captain R. F. Phillimore, were sister-ships completed in 1908. The first of Fisher's dreadnought battle-cruisers, they had the high speed for vessels that displaced 17,250 tons of 25 knots, for which they had to accept armour no thicker than that of an armoured cruiser; but they carried a modern battleship's armament, eight 12-inch guns, and batteries of 4-inch weapons to repel torpedo-boat attack. The *Inflexible* had been long in commission; she was in the Mediterranean when war broke out, joining the Grand Fleet in September after the unsuccessful pursuit of the *Goeben*. But mobilisation had caught the *Invincible* in dockyard hands having her experimental, electrically operated turrets converted to the well-tried hydraulic system. Though she had taken part in the Heligoland Bight action on 28th August, she still carried representatives of Messrs Vickers on board to ensure that her turrets worked satisfactorily and to complete fitting her for director firing. This possible handicap excepted, the two ships were immeasurably superior to von Spee's victorious East Asiatic Squadron. And, when they left England on the evening of 11th November, it was in compliance with these orders from the Admiralty:

23 *Victor of the Falkland Islands: Vice-Admiral Sir Doveton Sturdee*
From a study for a painting by Sir A. S. Cope

24 *The British armoured cruiser* Carnarvon, *Rear-Admiral Stoddart's flagship at the Falklands*

25 *Sturdee's flagship, the battle-cruiser* Invincible; *the* Inflexible *was a sister-ship*

On leaving Devonport . . . proceed to . . . South American waters. On passage to St Vincent it is possible you may receive orders by wireless to proceed to the West Indies, should information be received that *Scharnhorst* and *Gneisenau* are proceeding northward on Pacific Coast. Your presence in the West Indies would be necessary to provide for the contingency of the German squadron passing through the Panama Canal. Your main and most important duty is to search for the German armoured cruisers *Scharnhorst* and *Gneisenau* and bring them to action. All other considerations are to be subordinated to this end. . . .

The orders went on to place Stoddart's force under Sturdee's orders and gave him authority over all other commanders-in-chief when dealing with the German squadron. They suggested that, after coaling at St Vincent, he should make for the Abrolhos Rocks. But there were two important omissions: nothing was said about the need for haste, nor was the importance of secrecy mentioned; on the contrary, Sturdee was instructed: 'On your passage . . . you should communicate [by wireless] with H.M.S. *Bristol* and withdraw her and the *Macedonia* from the search for S.M.S. *Karlsrühe* and employ them in the operations against the German squadron.'

Since Sturdee assisted Jackson to draft these instructions for Fisher's signature, it could be argued that he was sufficiently aware of the need for both haste and secrecy for it to be unnecessary to specify either. Before, however, dealing with the consequences of these omissions, the other action taken by the Admiralty to counter the threat presented by von Spee after Coronel must be briefly recorded. Every foreseeable possibility was guarded against. Powerful Japanese squadrons were deployed at Suva and the Caroline Islands to cover Australia and New Zealand, whilst Patey took the *Australia* to join the Allied ships already off the west coast of North America. The *Defence* was to join the *Minotaur*, *Dartmouth* and *Weymouth*, and the old battleship *Albion* at the Cape; the South African Government's expedition against German South-West Africa, which was about to be launched, might prove a magnet that would attract von Spee to Luderitz Bay; indeed, for this reason the sailing of the expedition was postponed for a fortnight. West African waters would be guarded by the pre-dreadnought *Vengeance*, the armoured cruisers *Warrior* and *Black Prince* and the cruisers *Donegal*, *Highflyer* and *Cumberland*. Finally, the old battleship *Glory* and the cruisers *Berwick*, *Lancaster* and *Condé* (in addition to the already mentioned *Princess Royal*) were sent to watch the Caribbean. 'Thus,' wrote Churchill, 'to compass the destruction of five warships, only two of which were armoured, it was necessary to employ nearly thirty, including twenty-one armoured ships, for the most part of superior metal, and this took no account of the powerful Japanese squadrons, and of French ships or of armed merchant cruisers, the last-named effective for scouting.'

In the event, none of these world-wide movements was of comparable importance to those which took place off the east coast of South America. The concentration ordered off Montevideo did not prove wholly practicable. After leaving Lomas Bay the *Glasgow* and *Canopus* received a signal from the Admiralty

> to say that we were to proceed direct to Montevideo and *to avoid the Falkland Islands at all costs*. We came to the conclusion [wrote one of her officers] that they had good reason for this, and that the Germans were coming there, if they were not already there. Well, we could not go on for want of coal and the *Glasgow* partially crippled, so we simply had to come here [Port Stanley] and get coal as quickly as possible. We arrived on the Sunday forenoon and coaled and left at night, fully expecting to meet the Germans outside. We sent the *Glasgow* on ahead because she was being kept behind by our slow speed. The sea was still rough as it nearly always is here. That night was a very anxious one, we couldn't have fought our main deck guns and our forward 12-inch were full of water. However, nothing untoward happened. We had machinery defects and had [signalled] the Admiralty saying we must have five days to repair them: we had steamed about 18,000 miles and had been nearly always at sea except when coaling. Consequent on the [signal] saying 'avoid Falkland Islands', we had to risk breaking down and to try to reach Montevideo. [But] after we had steamed about 700 miles, about two-thirds of the way to Montevideo, we got a [signal] from the Admiralty:
>
>> '*Canopus* to remain in Stanley Harbour. Moor the ship so that your guns command the entrance. Extemporize mines outside the entrance. Be prepared for bombardment from outside the harbour: send down your topmasts. Stimulate the Governor to organise all local forces and make determined defence. Arrange observation stations on shore to enable you to direct fire on ships outside. Land guns or use torpedoes to sink a blocking ship before she reaches the narrows. No objection to your grounding ship to obtain a good berth. . . . Repair your defects. . . .'

By the 16th Grant, whose ship returned to Port Stanley on the 12th, could report:

Canopus . . . is moored head and stern to cover entrance of harbour and obtain fire to south-east over land. Engine-room repairs are now in hand. Possible landing places are now protected. Naval ratings, guns, 12-pounders are now being landed. Look-out and signal stations have been established. All battery positions and stations are now in telephonic communication. Entrance to Port William harbour will be mined shortly. Landing force marine detachment 70 men and local volunteer force of 150 men all under command of Captain R.M. Every assistance has been rendered by the Governor, Falkland Islands, and local administration.

But the Admiralty's sense of urgency was not matched by von Spee; the German squadron had only just sailed from Mas a Fuera.

The *Glasgow* reached English Bank on the 11th, where she met the *Cornwall*, Captain W. M. Ellerton, and *Defence* (Stoddart's flagship). The *Carnarvon*, Captain H. L. Skipwith, and *Orama* were in the vicinity. When the force sailed next day, Luce's ship was sent in to Rio de Janeiro where the Brazilian authorities, exasperated by the Germans' disregard for neutrality, allowed her to remain five days whilst her action damage was repaired in the Government floating dock, all charges being waived, a remarkable gesture of benevolence towards a unit of a defeated fleet by a country in which German influence was strong. The remainder of Stoddart's squadron joined the recently commissioned armoured cruiser *Kent*, Captain J. D. Allen, and the A.M.C. *Edinburgh Castle* at anchor off the Abrolhos Rocks on 17th November.

On the same day, six out from England, the *Invincible* and *Inflexible* reached St Vincent and began coaling, a slow business with the limited facilities available, 24 hours elapsing before they were ready to sail again. Neither the Admiralty nor Sturdee seem to have appreciated one consequence of this call at a Portuguese (neutral) port where several German merchant ships were berthed. Their captains might have realised the potential importance of a southward move by two such powerful ships and reported it to Berlin. They didn't do so, but the Western Telegraph Company's cable operators passed the interesting news to their opposite numbers in South America. In contrast, Sturdee was disturbed to hear French wireless stations in West Africa using Allied warships' commercial (non-secret) call-signs; and he signalled his two ships: 'The utmost harm may be done by indiscreet use of wireless. The key is never to be pressed unless absolutely necessary', though it was difficult to impress strict wireless discipline upon operators accustomed to 'chat' with each other on the ether, more especially when a shore station passed a signal to the *Invincible* of no greater importance than the news that one of her officers had become a father. Nor was this precaution of much strategic value when Sturdee stopped to examine merchant ships as he crossed the Atlantic, one of which might have subsequently reported the battle-cruisers; moreover he used the *Invincible*'s wireless on 23rd November to contact the *Edinburgh Castle*. It is not therefore surprising that, through one or other of these breaches of security, German agents in Montevideo knew by 24th November that Sturdee's flagship was off the Abrolhos Rocks. Very fortunately for the British admiral those agents, despite the undoubted efficiency of the German intelligence network, lamentably failed to appreciate the importance of the news. It was not telegraphed to Berlin; more important, nothing was done to advise von Spee except by a letter sent in one of the supply ships to Port Santa Elena, a rendezvous the German admiral was not destined to keep.

Montevideo's news was premature: the battle-cruisers, after visiting the Rocas Rocks in case the *Karlsrühe* might be found coaling there, did not join Stoddart's squadron, which now included the *Bristol* (still commanded by Captain Fanshawe) and the *Macedonia*, at Abrolhos until 26th November. In the lee of these barren islets, uninhabited except for the Brazilian lighthouse-keepers, where shoals provided an anchorage outside territorial waters, the big ships spent 48 hours coaling and transferring stores, whilst Stoddart shifted his flag to the *Carnarvon* so that the *Defence* could sail for the Cape. And Luce of the *Glasgow* called on his new admiral to press him to take the British force south to the Falkland Islands with all possible speed, advice which Sturdee disregarded in the light of the fresh instructions which he now received by signal from the Admiralty:

> *Scharnhorst*'s squadron was at Mas a Fuera . . . on 15th instant; later evidence which is less reliable, points to their presence in [St Quentin] on 21st. Proceed south with colliers and whole squadron. . . . Use Falkland Islands as main base for colliers. After coaling proceed to Chilean coast, avoiding letting your large ships be seen in Magellan Straits. Search the Straits inlets and channels taking colliers with you as necessary. *Australia* with Japanese squadron will arrive Galapagos Islands about 2nd December, and will move south should Germans remain in south. A powerful Japanese squadron is collecting at Suva, Fiji and will probably proceed to Marquesas Islands. . . .

This signal stressed, for the first time, the need for keeping secret the presence of the battle-cruisers in South American waters. As one result, Sturdee arranged for the *Glasgow* or *Bristol* to transmit any messages he had to send, since their presence in the area was already known to the enemy, a fortunate precaution when, for example, the squadron lost touch a week later with one of its units and Sturdee had to use wireless to locate her. On the other hand, the Admiralty signal said nothing about proceeding *with despatch*, an omission that might have had most unfortunate consequences. If the St Quentin intelligence was correct, von Spee could be expected to round the Horn by the end of the month. But Whitehall did not yet accept that this was von Spee's intention; moreover they believed that Sturdee already understood the need to hurry and so would arrive at the Falkland Islands by 3rd December (until he told them otherwise in a signal made on his departure from Abrolhos which was received on 30th November but neither Churchill nor Fisher then saw any need to 'give him a prog'). This was possible, but it wasn't Sturdee's way; though his ships could have made good 16–18 knots, he preferred 10 in order to husband his fuel and to search for enemy shipping as he steamed south. Moreover, when he rightly afforded an opportunity for his force to carry out battle practice, the target towing wire fouled one of the *Invincible*'s propellers: Sturdee then stopped his whole squadron whilst divers cleared it instead of allowing them to proceed and catching them up, which delayed their passage by a vital 12 hours.

Since the British force did not, therefore, arrive at the Falkland Islands until 7th December, four days later than the Admiralty's estimate, it was fortunate that Fate and von Spee played into Sturdee's hands in other ways. Not only did the German squadron remain at St Quentin until 26th November but, as they sailed south, the squadron ran into very bad weather. One of the *Leipzig*'s officers wrote:

The storm and sea grew steadily more violent. We sheered out of the line because [our] position was beginning to get dangerous. The heavy seas had shifted the deck cargo and all the shoots and scuppers got stopped up with coal so that water could no longer escape. At times there were three feet of water on deck and we were in imminent danger of capsizing. We turned up into the wind, so as to have our bows to the sea, and the danger was for a time averted. All hands had to turn to and shovel coal overboard. . . . The men were standing all the time waist deep in water . . . which was very cold. The *Scharnhorst* stood by . . . in case of need. By 1000 the worst was over. We steamed after the other ships. The *Dresden* also threw coal overboard. . . . The other ships had to do so as well. Towards evening the weather improved a little, but in the night the storm came on again. . . . The weather began to get better on the 28th, the wind gradually falling and the sea getting more calm. Finally, only a slight swell remained. . . . We had the dreaded Cape Horn on our beam on the night of 1st December. . . .

And next afternoon, whilst carrying out gunnery practice, von Spee sighted the British barque *Drummuir*. Finding that she carried nearly 3,000 tons of coal, and having been informed that the *Dresden* now had insufficient remaining to reach Port Santa Elena, the admiral decided to anchor his squadron again, off Picton Island. There they stayed until the 6th whilst the cruisers topped up from the *Seydlitz*, the *Drummuir*'s cargo was transferred to the *Baden* and *Santa Isabel*, and von Spee's officers enjoyed shooting duck on the island. Yet this further delay would not have influenced events but for the decision which von Spee took whilst his squadron lay in this desolate glacial outpost of the South American continent. Calling a conference of his captains before weighing on 6th December, the admiral informed them that intelligence confirmed the continued absence of British warships from the Falklands area. He therefore proposed to attack the islands in order to destroy the wireless station and coal stocks, and capture the Governor in retaliation for the British imprisonment of the Governor of Samoa. The operation would be carried out by the *Gneisenau* and *Nürnberg*, covered by the rest of the squadron.

Fielitz, his chief of staff, and von Schönberg of the *Nürnberg* were strongly in favour of this project; but Maerker of the *Gneisenau*, Lüdecke of the *Dresden* and Haun of the *Leipzig* thought it a strategical error. They doubted the news that Stoddart's ships had sailed for South Africa; they thought the squadron should pass the Falklands well to the east and appear without warning off the Plate. There can be no doubt that they were right. The damage the squadron could do to the Falklands was not worth the risk, especially since it must disclose the Germans' presence in the South Atlantic. If von Spee was to take any action against the Allies before attempting to run for home, he should have proceeded to the Plate area, which would have paid rich dividends. But the whole of his war career shows that attacks on trade were, to him, the least important aspect of cruiser warfare: it did not align with his offensive spirit. In the Pacific he had attacked enemy bases and enemy warships; if his squadron was to live up to the glory it had already gained, it must attempt the same pattern in the Atlantic.

Next morning, the 7th, having received a further signal from a German agent to the effect that Stoddart's squadron had left the

Falklands, von Spee confirmed his final fatal decision. And Maerker, despite his misgivings, issued the following orders:

> When *Gneisenau* and *Nürnberg* are detached . . . they will proceed at 14 knots to a point to the east of Cape Pembroke from which Stanley Harbour* can be overlooked. If the harbour is clear of enemy ships *Nürnberg* will reconnoitre as far north as Berkely Sound while *Gneisenau* off Port William lowers boats to sweep the entrance clear of mines. *Nürnberg* will then proceed in as far as Port Stanley in rear of boats and will embark stores and do destruction. *Gneisenau* will follow as far as the channel connecting Port William with Port Stanley. She will anchor there and send armed cutters to the town side under command of Lieutenant Kotthaus, who is to deliver an ultimatum to the Governor and try to bring him back to the ship. The cutters will be covered by *Nürnberg*. The two ships will rejoin the squadron not later than 1930.

When Maerker added a request to von Spee for a second light cruiser to support the operation, the admiral responded by signalling his force:

> From 0530 onwards *Gneisenau* and *Nürnberg* are to steer for a point five miles from Pembroke lighthouse; they are to reach this point by 0830. The main body will follow fifteen miles in their rear.

Von Spee also wirelessed the colliers awaiting him at Port Santa Elena, notifying them that the squadron's arrival there would be delayed 24 hours.

Thus the die was cast that led the German admiral to his death: he had given the order to execute an operation which was not only a strategical blunder, but which could have been carried out a fortnight before if, after Coronel, he had displayed the sense of urgency which the situation demanded. It is, however, equally true that events would have taken a different course if Sturdee had responded to the urgency with which Churchill and Fisher had dispatched the *Invincible* and *Inflexible* from England, and arrived several days earlier at the Falklands. When neither admiral appreciated that time is vital in war, it might have taken Sturdee months to locate the German squadron he had been sent to

---

* Stanley Harbour is a bay divided into two anchorages by a narrow channel. Port William is the outer, deeper anchorage, Port Stanley the inner anchorage off the tiny timber-built town of Stanley (Pop. 1,000), capital of the Falkland Islands. Cape Pembroke, with its lighthouse, is the southern of the two points forming the entrance to Port William.

destroy. As it was, Fortune, which had for so long smiled on von Spee, chose to give Sturdee his golden moment less than four weeks after his departure from England. As Fisher acidly commented in 1919: 'No one in history was ever kicked on to a pedestal of fame like Sturdee. If he had been allowed to pack all the shirts he wanted to take, and if Egerton [Admiral Sir George Egerton, Commander-in-Chief Plymouth] had not been given that peremptory order, Sturdee would have been looking for von Spee still!'

Leaving the Abrolhos Rocks on 28th November, the battle-cruisers steamed south in the wake of Stoddart's cruisers which were spread on a broad front to intercept the enemy—von Spee's force if it had already rounded the Horn ('We are getting quite excited now and expect to meet the Germans on Tuesday next', wrote one of the *Carnarvon*'s midshipmen on Sunday, 29th November, though on 4th December this possibility was discounted by news that the *Prinz Eitel Friedrich* had been sighted off Valparaiso) and the A.M.C. *Kronprinz Wilhelm* which was believed to be operating off the Plate. The *Orama* followed as escort for the squadron's colliers. With the exception of these, which were not expected to arrive until the 11th, the force, proceeding on its unhurried way and, delayed by the already mentioned accident with the target-towing wire, reached the Falklands at 1030 on 7th December, to the immense relief of the Governor and Grant, who had been expecting the German squadron almost hourly since 25th November as the result of a false report that it had rounded Cape Horn.

Sturdee found the islands, whose people and scenery recalled to the *Invincible*'s and *Inflexible*'s companies the Orkneys they had so recently left, well prepared despite their previous defenceless state. The measures Grant had taken—beaching the *Canopus* and transforming her into a fortress by camouflaging the old battleship to blend with the colouring of the bleak moorland landscape, with observation posts ashore connected by telephone, laying an improvised minefield across the entrance to Port William, and landing her 12-pounders and a detachment of Royal Marines—these measures had been supplemented by the Governor, who had enrolled every able-bodied man into a local defence force and sent the women and children away into the hinterland. The Falklands were not, however, Sturdee's immediate concern; suddenly displaying the sense of urgency which he had previously lacked, although he believed von Spee to be still off Valparaiso, he decided that 'in order to reach the Chilean coast at the earliest possible date, all ships (should be) ordered in together, to remain only 48 hours', the Admiralty being informed that, as soon as they had coaled, the force would sail again for Chilean waters late on the 8th. So the light-draught *Bristol* and *Glasgow* went right into Port Stanley where the *Canopus* was beached, whilst the battle-cruisers together with the *Carnarvon* and the ill-fated *Monmouth*'s sisters, *Cornwall* and *Kent*, anchored in Port William. Only the A.M.C. *Macedonia* remained on patrol outside; the rest of the force began coaling—when von Spee's ships were only a few hours, steaming away, approaching at a steady 10 knots.

The Germans, indeed, sighted the islands as early as 0230 next morning, the day promising to be exceptionally fine and clear. (Gales and fog are experienced for more than two-thirds of the year in this bleak part of the world.) So at 0530 von Spee ordered his squadron to clear for action and raise steam for 18 knots, and signalled the *Gneisenau* and *Nürnberg* to proceed in execution of previous orders. But Maerker had not gone far from the flagship when he reported that shore bearings indicated an error in the squadron's reckoning; his two ships could not be five miles from Cape Pembroke until 0930. There was, however, no reason to suppose that the delay would affect the operation. Around 0830, Maerker sighted the masts of the wireless station, which he knew to be between Stanley and Cape Pembroke lighthouse, and a column of smoke to the east from a vessel (the *Macedonia*) entering the harbour; but he could see nothing of what lay beyond the intervening neck of land except for a thick black cloud of smoke from which he deduced that his ships had been sighted and the coal stocks were being fired, as had happened at Papieté. Not until 0900, when the *Gneisenau* and *Nürnberg* were less than 10 miles from Port Stanley, did Lieutenant-Commander Busche, who was stationed in the *Gneisenau*'s control position high up her foremast, make out the funnels and masts that told him there were warships in the harbour.

Maerker then knew that he had been right in his view that Stoddart's squadron had not sailed for South Africa. He was not, however, willing to believe the next report which came from his gunnery officer: across the low-lying neck of land which linked Cape Pembroke with Stanley, Busche saw tripod masts, four of them. But the possibility that there were a couple of dreadnoughts in the South Atlantic was something undreamed of even in the cautious Maerker's philosophy: Busche was curtly told that the nearest battle-cruisers were as far away as the Mediterranean. So whilst Maerker signalled von Spee that there were probably three British 'County' class cruisers, and one light cruiser, with possibly two larger ships like the *Canopus* in Port Stanley, the *Gneisenau* and *Nürnberg* steamed on towards their appointed position five miles from Cape Pembroke. 'We were to proceed to the Falkland Islands', wrote a member of the *Leipzig*'s crew. 'Our admiral was convinced we should not encounter any superior force there. But how bitterly we were to be disappointed. . . .'

5

8th December 1914

'It was an interesting fight off the Falkland Islands ... a
good stand-up fight, and I always like to say I have a great
regard for my opponent, Admiral von Spee. At all events he
gave me and our squadron a chance by calling on me the
day after I arrived. He came at a very convenient hour
because I had just finished dressing and was able to give
orders to raise steam at full speed and go down to a good
breakfast.'

STURDEE'S above quoted words from a speech which he made after
the war, recall Drake's reaction to the news of the approach of the
Armada: 'and he stooped, and finished the game'. Sturdee might lack
the quicksilver mentality needed for a successful Chief of Staff at the
Admiralty, but as commander-in-chief of a fleet he had the advantage
of another quality: 'no man ever saw him rattled'; 'he doesn't lose his
head or get excited'. The victory he gained over von Spee before the
sun went down on 8th December is as much attributable to the calm,
unhurried way with which he faced a potentially dangerous situation as
to the superiority of his squadron over that of the enemy. An admiral
less imperturbable of temperament might have fluffed this golden
opportunity of annihilating the only substantial German naval force
outside the North Sea. For by 0750 only the *Carnarvon* and *Glasgow* had
coaled, the two available colliers had been alongside the *Invincible* and
Inflexible since early in the morning watch, and the *Kent*, *Cornwall* and
Bristol had still to replenish their bunkers. Moreover, only the *Kent* had
steam at less than two hours' notice, whilst the *Cornwall* and *Bristol* each
had an engine opened up for repairs. So the British squadron could
hardly have been less ready for action when, at 0756, the *Glasgow* fired a
gun to draw attention to the signal flying from the *Canopus*'s masthead:
'Enemy in sight!'

At 0800 Sturdee heard the news which Grant had received by telephone from the lookouts on Sapper Hill: 'A four-funnelled and a two-funnelled man-of-war in sight SE steering northwards.' The British admiral could have little doubt that this portended the approach of von Spee's squadron, but he was neither perturbed nor did he hesitate. Quietly he gave orders for the *Kent* to weigh and proceed out of harbour, for the *Invincible* and *Inflexible* to cast off their colliers, and for all ships to raise steam and report when ready to proceed at 12 knots. Then there was nothing more he could do for the moment—except eat his breakfast. By 0845, however, he was on deck to see the *Kent* steaming towards the entrance from which the A.M.C. *Macedonia*, unfitted to engage a proper man-of-war, had been recalled. But it would be at least another hour before the battle-cruisers and the *Carnarvon* and *Glasgow* could weigh, and longer than that before the *Cornwall* and *Bristol* were ready, although Sapper Hill had reported smoke from two further groups of ships to the south, news which by 0900 was amplified into a total of seven vessels, five of them warships, approaching the island, of which two were less than eight miles away. Sturdee could thank the weather for giving him so much warning of the coming of the whole of von Spee's force: had it been misty he might have had less than half an hour's notice, which would have been too little for him to do anything before an equally surprised von Spee had turned tail and disappeared. But he had to face a possibility which also occurred to Churchill. 'I was working in my room when Admiral Oliver entered with the following telegram . . . from the Governor of the Falkland Islands . . .:

> Admiral Spee arrived at daylight this morning with all his ships and is now in action with Admiral Sturdee's whole fleet, *which was coaling.*

We had so many unpleasant surprises that these last words sent a shiver up my spine. Had we in fact been taken by surprise and, in spite of our superiority, mauled, unready at anchor?' Von Spee's force could close Stanley Harbour, overwhelm the *Kent* and rake the rest of the British squadron with gunfire whilst it was still in harbour and able to bring only a small proportion of its superior armament to bear, and do enough damage to prevent it pursuing the German ships before they had disappeared over the horizon. Sturdee prepared for this eventuality: he ordered the *Canopus* to open fire as soon as the *Gneisenau* and *Nürnberg* were within range, his battle-cruisers, when they had rid themselves of their colliers, to be 'ready to open fire at any moment', and the

Carnarvon to clear for action and 'engage enemy as they come round the corner'.

More than 20 tense minutes passed, pregnant with disaster for Sturdee's squadron, during which Sapper Hill reported, at 0920, that the *Gneisenau* and *Nürnberg* had trained their guns on the wireless station. Then, at a range of 11,500 yards, the reverberating roar of the first salvo from the *Canopus*'s guns fired at their maximum elevation was answered by the shrill cries of a myriad of circling seabirds—with an entirely fortuitous result. On the previous evening, one of her officers remembers

> word was passed that we would carry out a practice shoot the following morning to show Doveton Sturdee how we had overcome the problem of firing our 12-inch guns 'blind' over the land at a target out at sea. The after turret's crew, in order to get one up on their deadly rivals in the fore turret, crept out privily by night and loaded with practice shell. Next morning they found it was a real battle and there was no time to unload. The result of this naughtiness was very interesting; the *Gneisenau* was well outside our extreme range, and live shell from my turret, the fore turret, burst on impact with the water, while those from the after turret richochetted and *one of them scored a hit*.

When Maerker had sighted the *Kent* leaving harbour he had increased speed with a view to cutting her off, but the *Canopus*'s unexpected hit at the base of the *Gneisenau*'s after funnel made him turn sharply away to the east. As a result Grant ordered cease fire after the battleship's second salvo, whereupon the *Gneisenau* and *Nürnberg*, now flying battle ensigns, resumed their previous course towards the entrance to Port Stanley. This alteration had no sooner been completed, however, when Maerker received from von Spee the order: 'Do not accept action. Concentrate on course E by N and proceed at full speed.' So the *Canopus* did not fire again—but she had served her purpose; by 0930 the German admiral had turned his main force to the east and detached his supply ships to a rendezvous to the south-east. (Later they were ordered to return to Picton Island.) For two reasons he had chosen flight instead of seizing his one chance of avoiding nemesis by engaging the British squadron whilst it was still in harbour; he believed that there were two battleships present, the danger of whose fire had been shown by the salvoes from the *Canopus*; and he supposed his squadron to be faster than the British. Not until 1100, when all five German cruisers, roughly in line ahead in the order *Gneisenau, Nürnberg, Scharnhorst, Dresden* and *Leipzig*, were steering a south-easterly course and trying to attain 22 knots, did he realise that the British force included two *battle-cruisers* which must be able to overhaul him long before the sun went down. And by that time it was too late to remedy his mistake, unless by altering to a more southerly course he could find an enveloping mist.

In the British ships the engine-room staffs had made remarkable efforts, as indeed they were to do throughout the day. The *Glasgow* was the first to have steam, at 0945, and weigh. A quarter of an hour later, first Stoddart in the *Carnarvon*, then the *Inflexible* and *Invincible*, and finally the *Cornwall* steamed out to join the watching *Kent* beyond Cape Pembroke. And in response to such reports as the *Inflexible*'s, 'Enemy making off as fast as they can', Sturdee hoisted that most exhilarating of general signals: 'Chase!' The last to leave, at 1100, was the *Bristol* which had also been at long notice. But well before that Sturdee, from reports signalled by the *Kent* and *Glasgow*, and then by seeing for himself from the *Invincible*'s forebridge the five columns of dense smoke from ships hull down on the horizon, knew the true position—that, barring some wholly unforeseen circumstances, he had von Spee at his mercy. He had a greatly superior force and he had ships that should be able to steam five knots faster than his opponent's heavy cruisers when they were less than 20 miles away, so that he could bring them within range of the *Invincible* and *Inflexible*'s 12-inch guns well inside two hours when there remained eight hours before sunset with nothing to indicate any change in the prevailing almost perfect weather.

With the same unhurried calm with which he had faced von Spee's arrival, Sturdee recognised his tactical advantages and decided against seeking an immediate engagement. Since the smoke from his battle-cruisers when burning both oil and coal so as to attain their highest possible speed, made it difficult for him to see the enemy, he reduced to 24 knots, ordered the *Inflexible* to haul out on the flagship's starboard quarter, stationed the *Glasgow* three miles on his port bow where she could be certain of keeping the enemy in sight without coming within gun range, and instructed the *Kent* to drop back to his port beam. Soon after 1100 he reduced speed to 19 knots so that the slower *Cornwall*, which could only manage 22 knots, and *Carnarvon*, which could only steam at 20 and had dropped many miles astern, might have a chance to catch up. Having thus annulled his order to chase, he signalled at 1132 that ships' companies would have time for a meal before action was joined. They had left harbour in a great hurry; the *Invincible* and *Inflexible* had had too little time to remove the coal dust with which they and their crews had been begrimed when the enemy had been sighted. Officers and men would fight all the better for a meal in their bellies, just as they would stand a better chance of recovering from wounds if they could wash and shift into clean clothing. 'Picnic lunch in the wardroom', noted one of the *Invincible*'s officers. 'Enemy visible as five little spots with five small streams of smoke right down on the horizon.' Von Spee's officers and men also had time for their midday meal, though many of them realised that, since they had been led into the trap which Churchill and Fisher had so successfully set for them, it was likely to be their last.

Around 1130, Sturdee received news from the *Bristol*, which had only recently cleared Stanley harbour, that 'colliers or transports' had been sighted approaching Port Pleasant. The light cruiser was promptly ordered to take the *Macedonia* under her orders 'and destroy *transports*'. Since neither of these ships thus took any part in the main action it will be convenient to mention here that Fanshawe located the *Baden* and *Santa Isabel* at 1500. Overlooking the sentence in Sturdee's Fighting Instructions, 'The opportunity might occur to *capture* the enemy's *colliers*' (see below pp. 140–1), he chose to obey the letter of his admiral's signal. Although they carried valuable cargoes, he sank both colliers by gunfire, after taking off their crews, which occupied the *Bristol* and *Macedonia* until after 1900. And by that time darkness veiled the faster *Seydlitz* which had separated from her consorts and made off to the south-east, intending to comply with von Spee's order to make for the Picton Island anchorage. (Later, on learning the fate of the German squadron, she steamed for San José Bay from where she tried to communicate with the *Dresden*. When this failed, she made for San Antonio, arriving on 18th December, and there, a month later, the Argentine Government decided to intern her as an auxiliary warship of a belligerent power.)

Onboard the *Inflexible*, at 'about 1220 the skipper came aft [to the wardroom] and said that the admiral had decided to get along with the work. The men on deck cheered.' Seeing that the *Carnarvon* was still six miles astern, her speed having dropped to 18 knots, and realising that it would take him too long to come within range of the enemy if he remained with the 22-knot *Kent* and *Cornwall*, Sturdee decided 'to commence the attack with the two battle-cruisers and the *Glasgow* only. . . . Speed was therefore . . . gradually worked up to 26 knots, the chase being rapidly overhauled. At 1247 the signal "Open fire and engage the enemy" was made', and a few minutes later the *Inflexible*'s gunnery officer saw the *Kent* which was on our disengaged side [give] us some unauthorised cheers as we opened fire [at the *Leipzig* at the rear of the enemy line], and it certainly must have been a very pretty picture. A blue cloudless sky above with blue calm sea below, the atmosphere extraordinarily clear, the two battle-cruisers forcing their way through the quiet sea, white streaks at stern and the water boiling in their wakes, often higher than the after decks, masses of black oily smoke from the funnels, against which the many white ensigns showed up in striking contrast. Ever and anon the roar from the forward turret guns and heaving masses of dark chocolate-coloured cordite smoke tumbling over the bows; a long wait and tall white splashes growing out of the sea behind the distant enemy.

'Behind the enemy' because the British ships were still on a south-easterly course, with the Germans running parallel to them fine on their starboard bow. The battle-cruisers could, therefore, only bring two turrets apiece to bear which limited their fire to two-gun salvoes every half-minute. And with no aids to fire control except for a couple of short base rangefinders and the most elementary of rate and deflection calculators and range clocks, when they had opened fire at the extreme range of 16,500 yards, it was some 20 minutes before any of their shells fell close to their target.

But then von Spee realised that it could only be a matter of minutes before the lagging *Leipzig* received a damaging hit; he recognised, too, that his armoured cruisers could no longer hope to avoid action with their superior opponents. So he took a decision, tactically correct, but which, none the less, did him and his Service the highest honour. He determined to sacrifice himself and his two heavy cruisers in the hope that this would allow his light cruisers to get away and continue their task of harrying Allied trade. At about 1320 he signalled the *Dresden*, *Leipzig* and *Nürnberg* 'to leave the line and try to escape'. And as soon as they had swung away to a southerly course, he led the *Scharnhorst* and *Gneisenau* to the ENE and opened fire at the pursuing British ships. But Sturdee had more qualities than imperturbability; he had foresight, and he 'was an officer who had made a special study of tactics'. On the way south to the Falkland Islands he had ordered his ships to carry out full-calibre firings, in at least one case the first since the outbreak of war. And before leaving the Abrolhos Rocks he had issued Fighting Instructions on three typewritten sheets of foolscap which included these words:

> The maximum enemy squadron likely to be met consists of two arm-oured cruisers, three light cruisers and possibly some colliers. The main

duty of the battle-cruisers is to deal with the armoured cruisers. The British armoured and light cruisers should not seek action with the enemy's armoured cruisers in the early stages but, in the event of the enemy's light cruisers separating or trying to escape, make it their business to deal with them: . . . The battle-cruisers will seek out the enemy's armoured cruisers and engage them between 12,000 and 10,000 yards, closing to 8,000 yards as fire becomes effective. The armoured cruisers should avoid action with the enemy's armoured cruisers until either the latter have been damaged or, owing to a superior tactical position, their fire can be effectively used. . . .

Fanshawe might overlook a sentence in these instructions (which covered the *Bristol* and *Macedonia*'s encounter with von Spee's colliers) but not Luce, Ellerton and Allen. As soon as they saw the German light cruisers turn away, the *Glasgow*, *Cornwall* and *Kent* swung round to starboard in pursuit without signal from Sturdee. Stoddart, on the other hand, realised that the *Carnarvon* lacked the speed to catch them: since two British armoured and one light cruiser should be ample to deal with three German light cruisers, he would do best to comply with the penultimate sentence in the above quoted passage; so he continued to follow the battle-cruisers.

The battle was thus divided into two separate actions; to present it coherently, the *Glasgow*, *Cornwall* and *Kent* must be left pursuing the fleeing *Dresden*, *Leipzig* and *Nürnberg*, whilst the engagement between the *Invincible* and *Inflexible*, supported by the *Carnarvon* (though for the moment she was some 10 miles astern), against the *Scharnhorst* and *Gneisenau* is described. This double duel began with a chase on parallel easterly courses with the *Invincible* engaging the *Scharnhorst* and the *Inflexible* the *Gneisenau* at a range which Sturdee was able to bring down to 13,500 yards, whilst keeping both ships' six starboard guns bearing. But it was far from being a one-sided action, despite the great disparity in strength. The German 'firing was magnificent to watch, perfect ripple salvoes all along their sides. A brown coloured puff with a centre of flame marking each gun as it fired. . . . Their shooting was excellent; they straddled us time after time,' and, at 1344 the enemy's fire took effect on the *Invincible*. From this Sturdee realised that his intention to fight at a range within that of his own guns, but outside that of the enemy's until the latter had been effectively damaged, was being frustrated by the Germans having the lee position. The dense smoke made by the battle-cruisers was blowing towards the enemy and

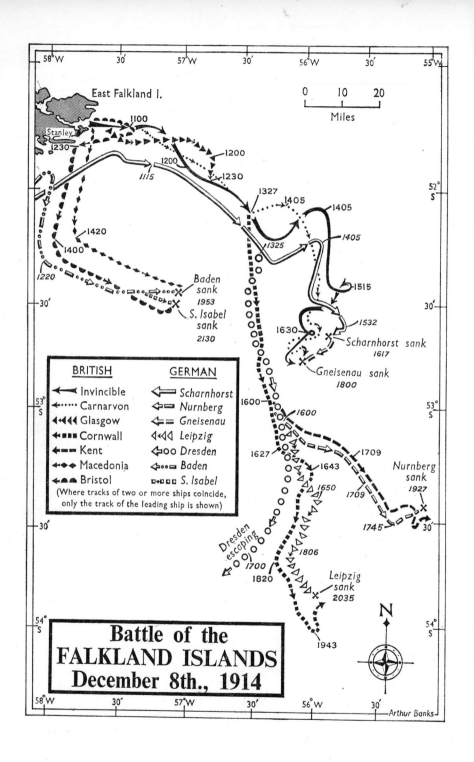

Battle of the
FALKLAND ISLANDS
December 8th., 1914

obscuring the British gunlayers' view of their targets and making spotting so difficult that hits were only a matter of luck. Sturdee could not know that the *Gneisenau* had already been struck twice, once below the waterline, and that the *Scharnhorst* had also suffered. And since he had no intention of giving the enemy a chance to cripple either of his battle-cruisers, he altered two points to port and opened the range so that from 1400 there was a lull in the action, whilst he tried to manœuvre the *Invincible* and *Inflexible* into a better position. But von Spee frustrated an attempt to get to leeward by a large alteration of course to the south: Sturdee could only haul round after him until, at 1445, he had closed the range enough to be able to open fire again. Von Spee, to his credit, did not parry this by a turn-away, but by a sharp alteration of course towards the British battle-cruisers, so that by 1455 the *Scharnhorst*'s and *Gneisenau*'s 9·2-inch guns could open fire at a range which came down to 10,000 yards, when Sturdee's ships were also engaged by their opponents' 5·9-inch weapons.

At this moment a full-rigged sailing ship, a beautiful sight with all canvas spread, appeared on the port beam. She was a Frenchman ignorant of the outbreak of war as she had left Europe in July. She went about to escape from the terrible spectacle before her. The consternation onboard at finding themselves in the middle of a naval battle in this out-of-the-way corner of the world after four months peaceful cruising is not hard to imagine.

The German fire was so effective—the Kaiser's crack gunnery ships had not lost their skill for all the odds against which they were fighting —that at 1515 Sturdee swung his ships through 32 points in an attempt to clear the smoke which fouled the range so badly, accepting the fact that this opened it to 14,000 yards. But when a splinter cut the halyards of von Spee's flag, causing Maerker to signal the *Scharnhorst*: 'Why is the admiral's flag at half-mast? Is he dead?', he received the reply: 'I am all right so far. Have you hit anything?' 'The smoke prevents all observation', Maerker answered, to which von Spee made a response characteristically generous and fatalistic that acknowledged Maerker's misgivings about the attack on the Falkland Islands: 'You were right after all.' But despite this apparently calm exchange of signals and the shortcomings of British shell which had been noted at Coronel, the weight of British metal, especially that filled with the recently introduced lyddite, was beginning to tell (each battle-cruiser's broadside weighed nearly 3,000 lb.; each German armoured cruiser's only 2,000 lb.). According to the German official history:

The heavier shells easily penetrated the casemate decks [of the German ships] and played havoc in the compartments below. . . . [Though] the explosive effect was less than one would expect from 12-inch shells . . . the damage increased continually, especially in the centre of the [*Gneisenau*]. The 5·9-inch casemates suffered severely and the wireless telegraph room was demolished. No. 1 boiler-room was flooded in consequence of a hit below the waterline and had to be abandoned; No. 3 boiler-room also began to fill. . . . Fires broke out in the unprotected parts of the ship fore and aft. . . . The efforts to put out the fires were aided by the mast-high splashes from shell that fell short, driving water through the shell-holes on to the decks.

The *Scharnhorst* suffered as severely; badly holed both forward and aft below the waterline so that she was drawing three feet more than normal, she could be seen to be on fire in several places, and by 1530 her third funnel had been shot away and her gunfire had slackened perceptibly, whereas the hits which had been obtained on the battle-cruisers had done nothing to reduce their fighting value.

Indeed, so many of the Germans' guns on their engaged side had been put out of action that von Spee swung his ships 10 points to starboard in order to bring their other broadsides to bear. But it was a move that allowed Sturdee to cross the enemy's wake and, at last to gain the lee position. Now, Sturdee wrote,

the effect of the [British] fire on the *Scharnhorst* became more and more apparent in consequence of smoke from fires and also escaping steam; at times a shell would cause a large hole to appear in her side through which could be seen a dull red glow of flame. Notwithstanding the punishment she was receiving, her fire was wonderfully steady, and accurate, and the persistency of her salvoes was remarkable.

As one result of the various alterations of course the *Invincible* and *Inflexible* had exchanged targets, but the latter ship's gunnery officer noted that

although our shots were obviously falling all over the *Scharnhorst*, [I] could not stop her firing: through the spray from short shots, one could see the 'twinkle' of her gun discharges, as she continued to fire the most perfect salvoes'. [*But there is a limit to what a well-built ship can stand, however admirable the discipline of her crew.*] I remember asking my rate operator, 'What the devil can we do?', when *Scharnhorst* suddenly shut up as when a light is blown out. We continued to fire on her for a moment longer and then she turned towards us and we could see that she was listing heavily, funnels all awry. As she was obviously sinking, we checked fire.

27 *Stanley Harbour on 8th December, 1914: the* Kent (left), Glasgow, Inflexible *and* Invincible (*with canvas snaked round her mast to confuse the enemy's rangetakers*) *getting under way*

28 *H.M.S.* Invincible *going into action at the Falklands, seen from the* Inflexible

29 *The Falkland Islands battle: the* Scharnhorst *and* Gneisenau (left background being engaged by the* Invincible (centre) *and* Inflexible

30 *H.M.S.* Kent *damaged by a shell from the* Nürnberg: *on left Sergeant Mayes, R.M.L.I., who was awarded the G.C.M. for saving his ship from destruction*

31 *The German armoured cruiser* Gneisenau

From the painting by T. H. A. Yockney

32 *Boats from the* Inflexible *picking up survivors from the* Gneisenau

33 *The German light cruiser* Dresden, *the only ship to escape destruction by Sturdee's force, flying the white flag of surrender at Mas a Tierra*

34 *The scuttled* Dresden *sinking*

35 *Survivors from the* Dresden *with Chilean seamen*

To quote Sturdee: 'At 1604 the *Scharnhorst*, whose flag remained flying to the last, suddenly listed heavily to port, and within a minute it became clear that she was a doomed ship; for the list increased very rapidly until she lay on her beam ends, and at 1617 she disappeared', five minutes after the *Carnarvon* had at last managed to catch up and add the fire of her 6-inch guns to the larger weapons of the two battle-cruisers.

There remained the *Gneisenau*, for which reason Sturdee gave no orders to his ships to stop and attempt to rescue survivors from the *Scharnhorst*, from which in consequence there were none. Maerker had already received one last signal from von Spee: 'Endeavour to escape if your engines are still intact', but 'the poor devils onboard must have known that they were doomed. The *Gneisenau*'s fore funnel was leaning against her second funnel and she had a large hole through her fourth one. Her foremast was all skewy, too.' The damage to her boiler-rooms had reduced her speed to 16 knots at which she tried to make away on a south-westerly course. The three British ships followed, trying to steam in single line ahead in the order *Invincible*, *Inflexible*, *Carnarvon*, all engaging her at ranges of the order of 10,000 yards; but so dense did the smoke lie across the battle area that they had as much difficulty in maintaining this line as they had in observing their gunfire. Indeed, around 1700, Phillimore, in a desperate attempt to clear it, turned 16 points and engaged the enemy on the opposite course before resuming the original one.* The battered, blazing *Gneisenau*, though under a hail of fire from three ships on different bearings, continued to fight on with such of her guns as remained in action, and at 1715 secured a hit—her last—on the *Invincible*'s armour belt.

> At 1730 [Sturdee reported] she turned towards the flagship with a heavy list to starboard and appeared stopped, with steam pouring from her escape pipes, and smoke from shell and fires rising everywhere. About this time I ordered the signal 'Cease fire', but before it was hoisted the *Gneisenau* opened fire, and continued to fire from time to time with a single gun [*the only one that had not been put out of action*]. At 1740 the three ships closed in . . . and the flag flying at her fore-truck was

* The chance that some of the *Invincible*'s stokers, on deck for a breather and knowing nothing of the tactics of the battle, saw their sister-ship apparently steaming *away* from the battle, gave rise to a regrettable lower-deck yarn to the effect that the *Inflexible* had run away. This led an infuriated Phillimore to ask for a court-martial to clear his name, but Sturdee, emphasising that he wholly approved the *Inflexible*'s conduct in the battle, sensibly refused to agree.

apparently hauled down, but the flag at the peak continued flying. At 1750 'Cease fire' was made.

We closed the *Gneisenau* which was then listing heavily and sinking [wrote the *Inflexible*'s gunnery officer]. She went over slowly and gave ample time for uninjured men to get on deck before the ship turned over on her beam ends. In this position she remained for about ten seconds and then [at 1800] quietly disappeared from view. There was no explosion, but steam and smoke continued to rise from the surface and hung in a thin cloud over the spot where she sank. Within a few minutes we were up to the survivors, some 200 men supporting themselves with hammocks, belts, spars, etc. *Carnarvon* and *Invincible* joined [*Inflexible*] speedily [in the work of rescue].

The *Gneisenau* had expended all her ammunition, lost steam from all her boilers and had had some 600 of her crew killed and wounded. Maerker had therefore given orders to scuttle the ship by flooding through the submerged torpedo tubes, and for all who could to save themselves.

[He] called for three cheers for His Majesty and the ship was then abandoned. I [wrote one of his officers] slipped down from the bridge on the port side, but fell into the water on the starboard side, the ship having suddenly capsized. When I came to the surface, I saw the forepart of the ship rise up again keel uppermost about thirty yards away. There were four men sitting on the torpedo tube, waving and singing, and presently the ship disappeared for the last time, carrying them down with her. Men clinging to objects around me were singing the 'Song of the Flag' and other patriotic songs. One man gave three cheers for the sunken ship, and the cheers were repeatedly taken up by others. I estimated that there were 270 to 300 men in the water. The temperature of the water was only 39° F., and during half-an-hour's immersion many of my companions perished. I and twelve others were clinging to a hammock and a round beam of wood. . . . We were all picked up by the *Inflexible*. I was amazed at the spirit displayed by the men . . .

—the same spirit which had enabled the officers and men of the proud *Scharnhorst* and *Gneisenau* to fight to the end against overwhelming odds, in an action in which Admiral Graf von Spee, victor of Coronel, himself went to a brave and honourable death, for all that the battle was as much due to his own mistakes as it was to the rapid dispatch of strong British reinforcements to counter the threat which his entry into the Atlantic presented to maritime trade. But the British ships had fought as well; Sturdee had proved his reputation as a tactician; the guns' crews of the battle-cruisers had kept up the fire from their heavy turrets for many hours, overcoming the very few breakdowns that occurred and maintaining the ammunition supply even when it was all but exhausted in some turrets, whilst their engine-room crews had achieved speeds in excess of those for which the ships had been designed. The destruction of the German armoured cruisers might have seemed inevitable, but it was not achieved without the skill and steadiness in action for which the British Navy had long been famous. Sturdee could well say to his cipher officers soon after the fight was over, 'Well, gentlemen, that was one of the most decisive actions you'll ever experience', for although fortune had presented him with more than one trump card, he had played them with outstanding skill. He could with justice remark to his flag captain that evening, 'Well, Beamish, we were sacked [*sic*] from the Admiralty, but we've done pretty well.' And throughout the action, which he had controlled from an exposed platform just below the *Invincible*'s fore top, not the safety of her conning tower, he had remained the calmest man onboard. Indeed, one of the ship's officers recalls that only once during the whole of that eventful day was the admiral ruffled: when the *Carnarvon* was slow in lowering her boats to help the battle-cruisers pick up the *Gneisenau*'s survivors, he twice signalled her to 'lower all your boats at once'.

> Now came the most awful part of all [wrote one of the *Carnarvon*'s midshipmen], rescuing the survivors who were in the water. When I say that the water was about 46° F. and the air about 51° F., with an awful cold wind blowing, you can imagine how dreadful it was for them. We all lowered our boats. . . . We got two cutters and a whaler out, and they managed to pick up forty. It was awful when they got back to the ship as a great many were wounded and some were half dead with cold. To make matters worse, our whaler was smashed against the ship's side, and our men and the Germans were in the water again. Fortunately, one of our cutters was near and managed to rescue all our men, but some of the Germans floated away calling for help which we could not give them. It was shocking to see the look on their faces as they drifted away and we could do nothing to save them. A great many were drowned. . . . We could see them floating past, a horrible sight.

A more senior officer in the *Inflexible* wrote:

> We got about fifty onboard as did two other of our ships.* We rescued their commander and about six other officers. The Germans in the

---

* The actual number of officers and men rescued were: *Invincible*, 108; *Inflexible*, 62; *Carnarvon*, 20 (including an officer who was related by marriage to Stoddart, such are the strange fortunes of war).

water were all waving their arms and shouting—not because they wanted to be saved any quicker, but because they had been told to do so, so as to keep them warm. We were busy getting out clothes, etc. for them, and by dinner-time we had several dining in the mess, and very nice fellows they are, too. They cannot give their parole as it is not permitted by their regulations; but there were so few that we gave them a good deal of freedom. Most of them could not sleep that first night, the scenes in their ships were so terrible. To see one's best friend suddenly torn to bits, or rush on deck one huge wound covered with blood and just have time to send his love home, is terrible. Although there was practically no damage to be seen, it was impossible for them to get from one end of the ship to the other, there was no upper deck or main deck left at all, and the lower (armoured) deck was full of holes and very hot. That is the result of long-range plunging fire. But we were all good friends after the fight, and both agreed that we did not want to fight at all, but had to. Over 2,000 of them must have been killed or drowned, with all their cherished possessions and their good ships. But they fought magnificently, and their discipline must have been superb.

The wardroom officers of the *Inflexible* were not alone in their chivalrous treatment of their prisoners. That evening Sturdee signalled to Commander Pochhammer, the senior surviving German officer:

The Commander-in-Chief is very gratified that your life has been spared, and we all feel that the *Gneisenau* fought in a most plucky manner to the end. We so much admire the good gunnery of both ships. We sympathise with you in the loss of your admiral and so many officers and men. Unfortunately the two countries are at war; the officers of both navies, who can count friends in the other navy, have to carry out their country's duties which your admiral, captain and officers worthily maintained to the end.

Sturdee received the equally chivalrous reply:

In the name of all our officers and men saved I thank your Excellency very much for your kind words. We regret, as you, the course of the fight, as we have personally learned to know during peace time the English Navy and her officers. We are all most thankful for our good reception.

Pochhammer behaved equally well when, after the battle-cruisers' return to harbour, Sturdee invited him to a small dinner party onboard the *Invincible*. At the end of the meal the admiral informed his guest that he was about to propose the traditional toast of 'The King', but that he would understand if Pochhammer preferred not to drink it. The

German commander answered that, having accepted Sturdee's invitation to dinner, he would conform with the Royal Navy's established custom which he knew well from pre-war days. It is, therefore, to be regretted that Pochhammer later chose to give his own version of this incident to the effect that when Sturdee proposed the loyal toast he had an overwhelming desire to throw his glass of port on the deck.

What damage and casualties had the British ships suffered in achieving this signal victory? The *Invincible*, which had borne the brunt of the enemy fire, had no man killed or wounded, though she was struck by 22 shells, the majority of 8·2-inch calibre. The resulting damage was little more than an inconvenience (the wardroom and a number of ratings' messes were wrecked), though enough to require the attention of a dockyard in due course, her fighting and steaming efficiency only being affected to the extent of one 4-inch gun out of action and one bunker flooded. The *Inflexible*, in contrast, only received three hits which killed one seaman and slightly wounded two others, but caused no significant damage, an important factor when she was so far from a dockyard. So Sturdee's decision to engage his opponent at long range had undoubtedly paid dividends—but only at an unexpected cost. The two battle-cruisers had each fired as many as 600 rounds, the greater part of their 12-inch ammunition, of which there were no stocks nearer than Gibraltar, so that they were in no condition to fight another battle with a ship larger than a light cruiser. But Sturdee is not to be blamed for this: only in the last decade had the Navy passed out of the era of close-range fire which had predominated for centuries, when more than 50 per cent of hits could be expected. No one had studied ballistics sufficiently to appreciate the inherent inaccuracy of guns at long range, and the consequent spread of a plunging salvo against which the danger space presented by a target is so small. Nor had peace-time practices disclosed the difficulties of laying guns in ships proceeding at high speed which caused so much vibration to gunlayers' and trainers' telescopes as well as obscuring them with spray. Nor had they revealed the baffling effects of smoke which hid the target from the gunlayers and made it impossible for control officers to spot the fall of shot. Nor had the inadequacy of the available fire control instruments to cope with the movements of a target that was being chased, which made it as difficult to keep shots in line as it was to find the range, been appreciated.

Not until much later in the war would it be realised that long-range gunnery had reduced the rate of hitting to something like five per cent. So it was fortunate for Sturdee that he had no reason to expect an encounter with anything larger than a light cruiser when he had disposed of the *Scharnhorst* and *Gneisenau*: the *Dresden*, *Leipzig* and *Nürnberg* were his only concern.

How had the *Kent*, *Cornwall* and *Glasgow* fared in their pursuit of these ships? Had Sturdee been premature in describing the result as so decisive? When, soon after 1300, von Spee ordered his light cruisers 'to leave the line and try to escape', all three had swung to starboard on to southerly courses. They might have been better advised to choose widely different ones, but von Schönberg and Haun shared Lüdecke's view that their best hope of escape lay in reaching the waters of Tierra del Fuego, where they should be able to replenish with coal. The *Dresden*, though nominally only a knot faster, soon drew ahead, whilst the *Leipzig*, whose engines and boilers were suffering even more than the *Nürnberg*'s from the wear and tear of many months' service in the Pacific, began to lag behind. On turning to chase them, the *Kent* found herself in the port wing position, with the *Cornwall* in the centre and the *Glasgow* to starboard. So Ellerton signalled his brother captains: 'I will take centre target (*Leipzig*) if *Kent* take left (*Nürnberg*) and *Glasgow* right (*Dresden*).' But though the *Glasgow* was able to steam faster than the two armoured cruisers, Luce, who was senior officer, soon had to express a different view: 'I fear I am gaining very slowly (on the *Dresden*)', he signalled Ellerton. 'Having already engaged *Leipzig* I feel I must stand by you.' Luce not only doubted whether the *Glasgow* could overhaul the *Dresden* before dark; he feared that the *Cornwall* might not be able to catch the *Leipzig*; and, even if she did, he knew from personal experience the vicious bite of her guns. So his first duty was to fight a delaying action with the *Leipzig* until the better protected *Cornwall* could come within range and her heavier armament deal decisive blows. Luce therefore slowed down slightly so as not to draw too far ahead of Ellerton, and at 1450 opened fire on the *Leipzig* with his forward 6-inch gun at 12,000 yards. Deciding that his ship had small chance of escaping the *Glasgow*, Haun responded with an alteration of course that brought his 4·1-inch guns within range, to which Luce reacted with a turn that allowed his after 6-inch to engage the enemy.

Twenty minutes after fire had been opened the *Leipzig* received her first hit [wrote her navigating officer]. A 6-inch shell struck the superstructure before the third funnel . . . [and] passed through the upper

deck into a bunker which happened to be the one in use. This caused a
temporary diminution of the forced draught in Nos. 3 and 4 boiler-
rooms [*and so a reduction of speed*]. We succeeded in stopping up the
hole sufficiently well with blankets and a heavy tub filled with water.
Our fire was very severely hampered by the fact that only three guns on
the starboard side, and occasionally the aftermost gun on the port side,
were in action, [and] at such long range the salvoes followed each other
very slowly and observation was very difficult.

None the less, when Luce allowed the range to drop to 11,000 yards,
the *Leipzig*'s fire was accurate enough to deter him from closing to
within range of the *Glasgow*'s 4-inch armament until he was sure that
Ellerton could catch up. Thus the running fight continued for an hour
before the range dropped to 9,000 yards, when the *Glasgow* was hit
twice. Luce's tactics subsequently caused as much ill-feeling between
the men of the *Glasgow* and those of the *Cornwall* as that already mentioned between the *Invincible* and *Inflexible*, the *Cornwall*'s inferring that
the *Glasgow*'s lacked the guts to take on a German ship with a lighter
armament without their support. The criticism is unjust: Luce was as
right not to hazard his ship whilst waiting for the *Cornwall* to come
within range, as he was in his initial decision to engage the *Leipzig*. He
could no more know the extent to which the *Glasgow*'s fire was damaging her opponent—that one shell had started a serious fire aft which her
crew were unable to extinguish—especially since he saw her engage the
Kent with her opposite battery when Allen passed in pursuit of the
Nürnberg, than he could be sure that the *Cornwall* might be able to overhaul the *Leipzig* without his help.

The result of Luce's tactics, which was to have eventful consequences, cannot, however, be denied. Ellerton was able to give the
order to open fire at 1617, in plenty of time to deal with the *Leipzig*
before dark. But by then Luce was in no position to pursue the flying
Dresden: even if Lüdecke's ship had not been obscured by the mist and
rain which a rising breeze now swept across the scene, she had damaged
one of the *Glasgow*'s boilers, causing her to lose speed. Consequently
Luce had no chance of locating the *Dresden* before she finally made her
escape under cover of night. He cannot be held responsible, either, for
Haun's understandable decision to turn his whole attention to his
more powerful opponent and for continuing to fire at the *Cornwall* for
the remainder of the action—though with little effect.

At 1642 [the *Cornwall*, wrote Ellerton] hit her foretopmast and carried
it away, and at 1703 [I] turned to starboard . . . and poured in my whole

broadside [nine 6-inch guns]—range 8,275 yards. This, of course, had the effect of opening the range, so at 1713 I again turned to port to close. . . . The weather conditions were now becoming very difficult. . . . We were temporarily out of spotting range, but at 1727 we again opened fire at 10,300 yards. When we got in to 9,100 yards, and could observe that we were hitting, I again turned to bring the A arc to bear, and fired the broadside. . . . We were constantly hitting the enemy at this time and continued to do so. . . . At 1806 we were just over 8,000 yards. . . . It was observed shortly afterwards that the enemy was on fire.

But all this time the *Glasgow* was left unfired at, so that she suffered no further damage, though Luce gave Ellerton all possible support, first by engaging the *Leipzig* from the same side, and then from the opposite quarter.

As the two British ships gradually closed in, their fire became increasingly effective; but the enemy, though ablaze from where the mainmast had stood, and also on fire right forward, continued to engage the *Cornwall* until, at 1930, her gunnery officer,

> after making a tour of inspection of all the guns and finding no more ammunition, reported that [the *Leipzig*'s] means of defence were exhausted. Fires in the superstructure and in the compartments below it, made them untenable. . . . [So] Haun turned to his torpedo officer, Lieutenant Schwig, and said: 'Go ahead, it's your turn now' and . . . the starboard tube was cleared away. . . . Between 1950 and 1955 three torpedoes were loaded and fired . . . Every eye was fixed on the torpedo tracks but we obtained no hits, for the enemy kept out of range of our torpedoes. We had now expended our last weapon. . . .

Glasgow and *Cornwall* then ceased fire and approached near enough to see if the *Leipzig* had struck, but as her ensign was still flying Luce opened fire again at short range for a few minutes in order to finish her. There was no response: Haun had already given the order to sink his ship by opening the seacocks and removing condenser doors. In the words of his navigating officer:

> Immediately afterwards all hands were piped on deck. The survivors were mainly technical personnel with some of the guns' crews and magazine hands: they assembled on the afterpart of the forecastle, practically the only unencumbered deck space. Everywhere else lay heaps of ruins with bodies of the dead and dying upon them. The bearing of the men was splendid; several of the dying asked whether the

flag was still flying and were comforted by the assurance that it would be kept flying till the ship sank. . . . The whole after part of the ship was one huge flame. . . . The crew were all dyed yellow with the fumes of the lyddite shell. Those who were unhurt tried to find all the wounded . . . and helped them as far as possible to attach lifebuoys, swimming jackets, etc. The captain spoke a few words to the men and called for three cheers for His Majesty the Kaiser, and then the crew led by Leading Seaman Pohlman, sang the 'Song of the Flag'.

The results of the British ships' final broadsides fired at close range, though justified by Haun's refusal to surrender, were inevitably terrible; they

> played havoc among the crowded groups of men and caused frightful slaughter. Many men sought shelter behind the gun shields but were mown down in heaps by shell splinters that ricochetted from the conning tower. . . . [Others] decided to jump overboard and swim towards the enemy . . . but the cold water numbed them. None of them were saved. . . . Meanwhile the sea had risen and the ship began to roll. . . . Darkness fell and it became too misty to see the enemy. The survivors stood with the captain on the forecastle.

To them, at 2030, Luce signalled: 'I am sending boats to save life'; and Haun gave the order to abandon ship just as his ship heeled over to port and began to sink rapidly by the bows. As her starboard propeller rose high out of the water she disappeared with her flag still flying and her captain still onboard. 'I deeply regret', Ellerton wrote, 'that so gallant an officer was not saved.' Between them the *Glasgow* and *Cornwall* picked up only seven officers and 11 men: no more survived after so stoutly fighting their ship against overwhelming odds for nearly four hours.

Ellerton concluded his report with a tribute to the way in which the Germans had fought their ship: Luce said of his own officers and men: 'After our experiences on 1st November their one idea has been to wipe out the reverse to His Majesty's arms at which they had been present . . . and it is a source of much gratification to us that we have been able to take part . . . in the destruction of the enemy's squadron which had inflicted this reverse upon us.' The *Glasgow* and the *Cornwall* had sunk the *Leipzig* at very small cost; Luce's ship had received only two hits which caused the death of one man and wounded four; Ellerton's, though struck 18 times, had suffered no casualties and no damage worse than two flooded bunkers. But—and it is a substantial 'but'—the *Dresden* had escaped, and by the time the *Glasgow* and *Cornwall* had finished rescuing the *Leipzig*'s survivors, Luce and Ellerton had little idea of the course they should steer to catch her.

Nor, for that matter, did they know what had happened to the *Kent* and *Nürnberg*. Soon after 1800 Sturdee had broadcast the news that he had sunk the *Scharnhorst* and *Gneisenau* and called for news from his other ships. Fanshawe answered that the *Macedonia* was proceeding to Port Stanley with the crews of the two German colliers: he also asked for orders for the *Bristol* and was instructed to join the flagship. But there were no other replies to Sturdee's signals. He therefore decided to detach Stoddart to reinforce the *Orama* to cover the possibility that the British colliers from Abrolhos, which were now due at the Falklands on the 10th, might be attacked by one of the missing German cruisers, whilst he searched with the battle-cruisers towards the Horn and ordered the *Glasgow* and *Cornwall* to prevent the enemy from entering the Magellan Straits as soon as he heard from Luce, around 2130, that the *Leipzig* had been sunk. Early next morning, however, Sturdee learned that these British cruisers had expended nearly all their ammunition, and was reminded that the *Cornwall* was seriously short of coal: they were therefore diverted to Port William to replenish, from where he subsequently heard that the *Cornwall* would be unable to coal until she had effected temporary repairs to her flooded bunkers. Later, he thought it desirable to cover the possibility that the enemy might make for a harbour in the sparsely populated West Falkland Island and detailed the *Bristol* to search there. Finally, the *Invincible* and *Inflexible* ran into thick fog when approaching Staten Island during the afternoon of the 9th, so that Sturdee judged that it would be useless to continue searching the Tierra del Fuego region and that, in view of a report from the *Glasgow* to the effect that a prisoner had stated that the 'German admiral's last orders to light cruisers were to make for South American east coast', he should sweep north. At the same time, he became seriously concerned at the continued absence of news from the *Kent*, so he ordered Luce to defer coaling and take the *Glasgow* and *Macedonia* out to search for her. Before they could sail, however, Allen's ship was suddenly sighted from Sapper Hill approaching Port Stanley, and after she had anchored at 1530, Sturdee received a signal which told him why he had had to wait 24 hours for news of the *Kent*. Allen's own report (here abbreviated) of his duel with von Schönberg gives a vivid picture of how his more powerfully armed and better protected, but nominally slower ship managed to catch the *Nürnberg*:

I steered directly after her, sending orders down to proceed at the utmost possible speed. The officers and men of the engine-room department made a most determined effort to overtake the enemy. All available wood, such as accommodation ladders, hen coops, wooden lockers, capstan bars, etc., was broken up and passed down into the stokeholds to be used in the furnaces. The stokers responded magnificently to my order for 'more speed'. The maximum horse-power of the ship was exceeded by 5,000, and the speed must have been at least 25 knots, an exceedingly creditable performance. Shortly after this the distance of the *Nürnberg* appeared to be decreasing, and at 1700 she opened fire on the *Kent* with her two stern guns and port after gun. I replied with a shot from the fore turret at extreme elevation, but [it] appeared to fall short. The first few shots from the *Nürnberg* went over the *Kent* and dropped astern, but the *Nürnberg* quickly found the range, about 12,000 yards, and from then onwards her shooting was remarkably accurate, her projectiles falling into the sea all round and quite close to the *Kent*. One shot hit the *Kent* on the starboard side aft, bursting on the upper deck. I fired two guns every few minutes at extreme elevation, to try and reach her, and altered course so as to bring the two foremost starboard guns to bear as well as the fore turret. The distance gradually decreased until she got within range of my guns at 1709, and I then fired salvoes continuously.

We now gradually closed until the range dropped to 7,000 yards, when the *Nürnberg* altered course eight points to port, bringing the whole of her port broadside to bear. I altered course to port, too, so [that] I succeeded in getting on her beam by the time the range had dropped to 6,000 yards [and] opened fire with all the starboard guns as soon as they would bear. We both steered for about a quarter of an hour on slightly converging courses until the range decreased to 3,000 yards, the *Kent*'s shooting [being] excellent; our shells were bursting all over the *Nürnberg*.

At 1802 [we both] altered course to starboard [and the] range gradually increased to 4,000 yards. She was now on fire forward, and her speed had decreased. At 1813 I crossed her bow at a distance of 3,450 yards, bringing all the starboard guns to bear on her when she was end on. I continued turning to starboard, and we were both steering for a short time on almost opposite courses. When she was about two points before my starboard beam I put my helm hard-a-starboard and got into a position on her starboard bow with all my port guns bearing on her. [She was now] practically stopped [and] at 1835 she ceased firing. On observing this I ordered 'Cease firing'.

I steamed towards her [until] I had closed to 3,350 yards [and] could see quite clearly that she was still flying her colours, and as she did not appear to be sinking I again opened fire with all guns. Five minutes later she lowered her colours. I immediately ceased firing and stopped. She now appeared to be in a sinking condition, as she was well down by the stern and had a list to starboard. I ordered all available boats to be got ready at once, and prepared for saving the survivors.

At 1926, [as] she heeled right over to starboard and slowly sank, I observed a small group of men on her quarterdeck waving a German ensign attached to a staff [*and through the windswept drizzle which threatened to obscure this sombre scene, Allen caught a glimpse of the white hull and bleached sails of the French vessel that had already been a mute witness of the battle-cruiser action*]. I then did my utmost to save as many men as possible. My three boats were all holed by fragments of shell and splinters, so the carpenters were ordered to repair the least damaged, a cutter and a gig, which were lowered after about twenty minutes. Altogether twelve men were picked up but only seven survived, the remainder being dead when brought onboard or dying shortly afterwards. [*Von Spee's son, Otto, was not among those rescued.*]

I remained in the vicinity till 2100, when it was nearly dark, then hoisted the boats and proceeded towards the Falkland Islands. I was unable to make any signals by wireless telegraphy, as a shell had passed through the office and damaged the transmitting instruments.

I regret to report that during the action four men were killed and twelve men wounded. The *Kent* was struck thirty-eight times altogether by the enemy's shell during the action [but] there is no serious damage to the ship. The total number of rounds fired was 646.

I very much regret if my closing the enemy to such a short range was the cause of so many casualties. If I erred in taking my ship too close to the enemy it was due to my extreme eagerness to sink her before she could escape [when] there were only a few more hours left before dark.[*In contradistinction to Luce, Allen was fully justified in taking his ship in to close range, as the* Kent *was armoured and could expect no support.*] I cannot sufficiently express my appreciation and admiration of the splendid behaviour of all officers and men under my command. From the time the enemy were first sighted until the end of the action, they have all fully acted up to the best traditions of the British Navy.

Only one fire occurred during the action, and that was in A3 casemate. A shell struck the gunport and burst; the flash must have ignited one or more charges inside the casemate, as a flash of flame went down the hoist into the ammunition passage. There was a charge at the bottom of the hoist at the time, but fortunately the man standing there, Sergeant Charles Mayes, R.M.L.I., had the courage and presence of mind to throw away the charge and flood the compartment, which prevented the fire spreading [*an act of heroism for which he was awarded the Conspicuous Gallantry Medal*]. There can be no doubt that the ship narrowly escaped being blown up as, had a charge caught fire in the ammunition passage, the flash would probably have set other charges on fire and reached the magazine before the watertight doors could have been closed.

I wish to express my admiration of the very gallant and determined manner in which the captain, officers and men of the *Nürnberg* fought their ship till she was sinking. They continued firing their guns with great accuracy and rapidity after their ship had been struck many times and when she was on fire. The courage and discipline of officers and men who put up such a good fight is unquestionable, and their gunnery and organisation must have been in a very high state of efficiency.

Thus, within six weeks of leaving the Admiralty Sturdee effectively fulfilled the task with which he had been entrusted. Surprised by the enemy in circumstances that would have rattled many another man and led him to make serious errors of judgment, he had scored a victory as decisive as any in British history—in his son's words, the last to be 'fought out in the old style, against a worthy foe whose force displayed splendid courage, determination and efficiency, between ships by gunfire alone, unaided by aircraft, in waters entirely free from mine-fields and submarines'. Recognising their superiority, the British ships had adopted tactics which had enabled them to sink four out of five of the German squadron which for the past four months had cast its menacing shadow over Allied operations in three oceans, without suffering significant damage or casualties themselves.

Churchill wrote to Fisher: 'This is your show and your luck. I should have only sent one greyhound [*i.e. battle-cruiser*] and *Defence*. This would have done the trick. But it was a mighty coup. Your flair is quite true', a gesture which the First Sea Lord acknowledged with the words: 'Your letter *pleasant.* . . .' None the less, the First Lord had no doubt about the measure of Sturdee's achievement: the consequences were

> far-reaching and affected simultaneously our position in every part of the globe [wrote Churchill]. The strain was everywhere relaxed. All our enterprises, whether of war or commerce, proceeded without the slightest hindrance. Within 24 hours orders were sent [from the Admiralty] to a score of British ships to return to home waters. For the first time we saw ourselves possessed of immense surpluses of ships of certain classes, of trained men and of naval supplies of all kinds and were in a position to use them to best advantage. The public, though

gratified by the annihilating character of the victory, was quite uncon-
scious of its immense importance to the whole naval situation.

Sturdee's achievement was as loudly acclaimed in the Allied capitals
as it was welcomed by the greatly relieved inhabitants of the Falkland
Islands: 'It is really a spanking victory', wrote the Governor's A.D.C.
'Last night H.E. had all the Volunteers and most of the so-called lead-
ing people of Port Stanley up to Government House for a drink to the
King and the Royal Navy.'

'I heartily congratulate you and your officers and men on your most
opportune victory', signalled King George V, to which the Admiralty
added: 'Our thanks are due to yourself and to your officers and men for
the brilliant victory you have reported.' And when the *Invincible* and
Inflexible returned to the Falklands to coal on 11th December, Sturdee
received similar signals from Jellicoe on behalf of the Grand Fleet and
from the French and Russian Admiralties, whilst at home many an old
shipmate, who had no idea that the admiral had gone to the South
Atlantic, sent their congratulations through Lady Sturdee, among
them Beresford:

> Please accept my warm congratulations on the splendid achievement of
> my old friend and chief of staff. How certain he was to distinguish
> himself if he got the chance and how clever of him to find out the enemy
> so quickly. He has fairly avenged the death of that splendid officer,
> Admiral Cradock. . . .

But in this first glory of his success Sturdee did not forget those
to whom he owed it—nor that the *Dresden* remained at large.

> This memorandum [he wrote to his captains] is to be read to your whole
> ship's company on the quarterdeck. The Commander-in-Chief wishes to
> congratulate all the ships of the squadron on the success of their main
> encounter with the enemy's squadron, and to thank the Rear-Admiral,
> Captains, Officers and Men for their individual assistance in attaining
> this great result. [*For which Prize Bounty totalling £12,160 was subsequently
> shared between the battle-cruisers and cruisers. Grant brought an action before the
> Prize Court to obtain a share for the* Canopus, *but he failed to establish his
> claim.*] The zeal and steadiness under fire of all hands was most notice-
> able. [But] the victory will not be complete until the remaining cruiser
> is accounted for, and directly the squadron is coaled a further organised
> search will be made. . . .

6

Checkmate

'Hardened steel are our ships,
Gallant tars are our men,
We never are wordy.
(Sturdee, boys, Sturdee)
But we'll quietly conquer again and again.'

From Punch, *16th December 1914*

BY 1700 on 8th December the *Dresden* had lost sight of her pursuers. A couple of hours later Lüdecke knew from intercepted wireless traffic that the *Scharnhorst, Gneisenau* and *Leipzig* had been destroyed and that nothing was to be heard from the *Nürnberg* so that, as in the first weeks of the war, he must act on his own. His immediate need was coal, but the German supply ships would not answer his signals. Since the *Baden* and *Santa Isabel* had reported being chased by British warships, he had to conclude that they were unlikely to comply with von Spee's order to return to Picton Island. Because he also thought that the entrance to the Magellan Straits would be guarded by the enemy, he altered course at dusk for a position well south of Cape Horn which the *Dresden* safely passed soon after midnight. Next morning she was off the entrance to Cockburn Channel, one of the multitude of inlets on the western side of Tierra del Fuego, and that afternoon Lüdecke anchored his ship in Sholl Bay, close under the forbidding slopes of Mount Lizzie.

Here he thought himself sufficiently safe from discovery to land parties of men to fell timber to augment the *Dresden*'s remaining 160 tons of coal. Unfortunately the Chilean destroyer *Almirante Condell* arrived on the evening of the 11th to draw Lüdecke's attention to the convention restricting a belligerent warship's stay in neutral waters to 24 hours. This left him with no alternative but to proceed to Punta Arenas, where the *Dresden* anchored on the afternoon of the 12th.

There Lüdecke found the local authorities, who had previously permitted H.M.S. *Otranto* to stay for 51 hours, willing to allow the *Dresden* to remain as long whilst she filled her nearly empty bunkers. As fortunately, the Chilean Government's instructions that the *Dresden* was not to be allowed to coal *at all* did not reach Punta Arenas until after she had sailed at midnight on the 13th. Lüdecke restricted his stay to 32 hours because he knew that his arrival at Punta Arenas would have been reported by the British consul, Captain Milward; the sooner the *Dresden* sought refuge where she was less likely to be caught by the enemy the better.

Sturdee had, indeed, received Milward's report very early on the 13th, and immediately ordered the *Inflexible*, *Glasgow* and *Bristol* to raise steam and head for Punta Arenas, under Phillimore's command. And later, at Stoddart's suggestion, he sailed the *Carnarvon* and *Cornwall* with orders to work down the coast from Port Madryn in case the *Dresden* should elude Phillimore's force and double back into the South Atlantic. Thus the hunt was up—but Sturdee was not to be in at the kill. On the 8th and 9th he had signalled first reports of the Falklands battle to the Admiralty, and on the 10th the failure of his ships' immediate search for the *Dresden*, adding that as soon as they had completed with coal he intended to divide his force into three squadrons, one to search all round Tierra del Fuego, another the east coast of Patagonia, the third the coast of Brazil. All, he added, had sufficient ammunition to deal with a light cruiser but not armoured ships. But the Admiralty could not allow two battle-cruisers to be retained for this service; Churchill and Fisher, who had so courageously accepted the risk inherent in withdrawing them from the Grand Fleet, agreed that they must return to home waters. Churchill, however, refused to accept Fisher's proposal that Sturdee should transfer his flag and remain to compass the *Dresden*'s destruction. The task did not merit the presence of such a senior flag officer; moreover, he realised the First Sea Lord's motive. Fisher, inwardly seething with anger at the praise being lavished on his *bête noir* from so many quarters, wanted to prevent Sturdee, for as long as possible, from enjoying the public acclaim he would receive as soon as he returned to England. Since the *Prinz Eitel Friedrich*, the ghost of the *Karlsrühe* and the *Kronprinz Wilhelm*, as well as the *Dresden*, remained to be located, Sturdee was ordered on the 13th to return to England with the *Invincible* and *Inflexible*, after dispatching the *Kent* and *Orama* to join the Allied force in the Pacific, and the *Canopus* to act as guardship at the Abrolhos Rocks, leaving the remaining ships to hunt the *Dresden* under Stoddart's command. When, however, the Admiralty heard that Lüdecke was not seeking internment at Punta Arenas as they first supposed, but was being allowed to coal, they signalled Sturdee early on the 14th that, whilst the battle-cruisers were wanted home as soon as possible, he was to use his discretion as regards dealing with the *Dresden*: 'Object is destruction not internment. . . . Press your chase.' Sturdee answered on the 15th that, though he himself intended to sail for England in the *Invincible* on the 16th, the *Inflexible* would continue to search for the *Dresden*, together with the *Bristol, Glasgow, Carnarvon* and *Cornwall* until the 29th, when she would have to return to the Falklands for coal. She, too, would then sail for home, leaving the cruisers to deal with the *Dresden* if, indeed, they had not already been successful. But this was not to be: Lüdecke had sought refuge in lonely Hewett Bay on 14th December, and there he remained whilst the British ships searched in vain for him in many possible hiding places in the waters of Patagonia and Tierra del Fuego, Milward doing what he could to help with intelligence despite the difficulties which the local Germans placed in his way.

Before Christmas Fisher's smouldering wrath took fire, and there began an exhibition of spite, always to be regretted in so great a First Sea Lord. On the 18th the Admiralty signalled Sturdee to return home at once with both battle-cruisers, and added: 'Report fully reason for the course which you have followed since the action. . . .' Sturdee might have gained a victory over the enemy but, as Fisher wrote viciously to Jellicoe on the 20th, his 'criminal ineptitude in not sending a vessel to Punta Arenas at the close of the action . . . has disastrously kept from you light cruisers now hunting *Dresden*, which ship was forced to Punta Arenas for coal on 11th December as she was empty'. But if Sturdee suspected that there was a sting in the last sentence of the Admiralty's signal, he did not show it in his reasoned reply whose sense has already been conveyed in these pages, to which he added that the *Inflexible* was being withdrawn from the search to follow the *Invincible* to St Vincent, where both battle-cruisers would replenish with ammunition. (He followed this signal with a fuller written report dated 24th December, but this did not reach London until the middle of January.) Their urgent need of this before they approached home waters was emphasised on the 20th when Sturdee received 'strong evidence . . . pointing to the possibility of the presence of the (German battle-cruisers) *Moltke, Seydlitz* and *Von der Tann* within wireless range of

Montevideo', so that he proposed to take the *Invincible* back to Port Stanley and concentrate there with the *Inflexible* and *Australia*. But this precaution proved unnecessary when, within a few hours, the Admiralty was able to assure Sturdee that they knew 'for certain that ships you mention were in the North Sea on 16th December'.

For a fortnight it seemed that Fisher had accepted Sturdee's explanation of his conduct after the battle. But on 3rd January the Admiralty abruptly signalled:

> Explain why neither *Inflexible*, *Invincible* nor any other vessel of your command proceeded immediately on completion of action to Punta Arenas to cable Admiralty and also to obtain information from British consul there in view of cessation of wireless communication with your squadron.

Sturdee answered briefly: 'Reasons for actions taken given in my [reply to your signal of 18th December].' Fisher retorted by repeating his enquiry, adding that the previous reply 'does not answer the question'. So this time Sturdee answered:

> *Firstly*: Report of action was passed by wireless through the Falkland Islands station to Montevideo and thence direct to the Admiralty. . . . If a ship had been sent to Punta Arenas the first report of the action could not have been dispatched to the Admiralty so early as it actually was. Further, under the twenty-four hour rule, the ship so sent would have had to leave before the *Dresden* actually arrived.
>
> *Secondly*: Punta Arenas had less information as to the movements of German squadron than I had been able to obtain.
>
> *Thirdly*: All indications pointed to the *Dresden* hiding for a time. This I understand she did in an uninhabited spot in Tierra del Fuego until discovered by the Chilean man-of-war *Almirante Condell* who ordered her to Punta Arenas.
>
> *Fourthly*: As it was anticipated that the [supply ship] *Seydlitz* had been with the German colliers, the neighbourhood of the Horn and the Falklands appeared to be the first place to examine until the ships had to return to coal and a regular search could then be organised.
>
> *Fifthly*: Both *Invincible* and *Inflexible* were required to sweep these large areas and I considered it unlikely that the *Dresden* would proceed to Punta Arenas.
>
> Their Lordships selected me as Commander-in-Chief to destroy the two hostile armoured cruisers and I endeavoured to the best of my ability to carry out these orders. I submit that my being called upon in three separate telegrams to give reasons for my subsequent action was unexpected.

Many another admiral would have phrased this protest in less moderate terms; none the less Sturdee received the tart rebuke: 'Last paragraph of [your signal] is improper and such observations must not be repeated.' Fisher did not, however, persist with his attacks: 'Their Lordships await your written report and dispatches before coming to any conclusion', completed this unedifying exchange.

The *Invincible*, having been diverted to Gibraltar for docking and action repairs, arrived there on 11th January. On the 16th Sturdee's report and written explanation of his subsequent actions reached the Admiralty. As soon as he had read them, Churchill was in no doubt that the victor of the Falklands was not open to serious criticism and merited another important sea appointment. On the 21st Sturdee received a signal from the First Lord to the effect that he was to take command of the Fourth Battle Squadron of eight of the Grand Fleet's dreadnoughts, as soon as he could return home, an offer for which he returned his thanks. But Fisher's vindictive spirit had not been quenched. When Sturdee reached London a fortnight later and reported to the Admiralty, the First Sea Lord kept him waiting for several hours before consenting to receive him, then restricted the interview to five minutes, during which nothing was said about Sturdee's success; he was only castigated for his failure to catch the *Dresden*, and for his protest at being three times called to task for it. Finally, having heard that Sturdee had been summoned to Buckingham Palace to give the King an account of the battle, Fisher tried to prevent him having this satisfaction by ordering him to leave immediately for Scapa Flow; but Sturdee insisted on deferring his departure for 48 hours.

Fisher's behaviour was repeated over the publication of Sturdee's report on the Falklands action in the *London Gazette*. This comprised a covering letter with his own detailed report and those of his ships' captains as enclosures. He understood the minor deletions made to these in the interests of security—the speed achieved by the British ships and their fire-control difficulties, to cite two examples—but he understandably protested at the extent to which his covering letter was doctored. These were Sturdee's words:

Invincible *Inflexible* *Carnarvon* *Cornwall* *Kent* *Glasgow*	I have the honour to report that at 0800 on 8th December, 1914, an attack on Port Stanley, Falkland Islands, was attempted by a German squadron consisting of two cruisers and three light cruisers accompanied by two colliers. The squadron (names in margin) which I have the honour to command was coaling in

Bristol
Macedonia

port at the time. H.M.S. *Canopus*, stationed in Port Stanley for its defence, opened fire with her 12-inch guns when the leading ships of the enemy came within sight and range over the low-lying land. This unexpected resistance and the simultaneous observation of the tripod masts of the battle-cruisers over the land caused the enemy to turn away at speed without opening the entrance to the harbour. The squadron weighed. A general chase ensued, followed by an action with the result that the ships named in the margin were sunk, the *Dresden* alone escaping.

Scharnhorst
Gneisenau
Leipzig
Nürnberg
Colliers:
Baden
Santa Isabel

It gives me great satisfaction to be able to report that I was most ably assisted by Rear-Admiral Stoddart and all the captains who, knowing my intentions, carried them out without further orders, thus reducing signalling to a minimum. The zeal and steadfastness under fire of all hands during the hotly contested action was most noticeable and has been brought to my attention by each captain. The officers and the whole engine-room department in every ship greatly distinguished themselves by their energy in meeting a sudden demand when, after long periods at sea, the ships of the squadron were coaling and overhauling machinery during the short time it was intended to remain in harbour. Where everyone did their duty according to the highest traditions of the Naval Service, it is not easy to individualise, but I attach a list of officers and men who showed merit.

I deeply regret the needless sacrifice of so many lives by an enemy who displayed such bravery, skill and endurance; after the ships were defeated and sinking and in no position to make any further defence, they did not surrender. Notwithstanding this, every practicable effort was made to save life. S.M.S. *Scharnhorst*, with the Admiral and all hands, sank in the middle of the engagement.

Since there can be no humanity on the public face of the enemy in modern war, the excision of the reference to von Spee's gallant fight is understandable; but only Fisher's determination to deny Sturdee, so far as he could, the credit that was his, can explain the substitution of the following brief lines for the whole of the above letter, without so much as the courtesy of informing him in advance:

I have the honour to forward a report on the action which took place on 8th December, 1914, against a German squadron off the Falkland Islands.

None the less Fisher never succeeded in seriously dimming the light of Sturdee's glory. Many were the letters he received like these:

The best news I have had yet has been your victory. . . . The fact that it was all done so promptly makes it a triumph for you and I rejoice in your success more than I can express. . . .

I don't know how to express all I feel about your most glorious victory. It's too splendid—and oh, if you knew what the whole Navy and the Nation are saying about it—it's just grand. It was all so complete and perfect. . . .

And the list of awards by His Majesty for the battle included a baronetcy for Sturdee, who was the first naval officer to receive this traditional honour for a successful action at sea since Captain Hoste's victory off Lissa in 1811. He remained in the Fourth Battle Squadron until February 1918, leading it at Jutland, which he deeply regretted did not result in the destruction of the High Seas Fleet. He then became Commander-in-Chief at the Nore; and, having received the thanks of Parliament for his war service and a grant of £10,000, reached the pinnacle of the profession to which he had given such long and distinguished service; in 1921 he was promoted Admiral of the Fleet, when, to his great satisfaction, he received letters in terms such as these:

I am so glad that at last you have received this, the one and only possible service or professional recognition of *the* successful action of the war. . . .

This seems to have put matters right and to have vindicated the dignity of the Service. . . .

He spent his last years as President of the Society for Nautical Research, actively sponsoring the scheme for restoring the *Victory* to her condition at Trafalgar and for preserving her in dry dock at Portsmouth. He died in 1925, shortly before his 66th birthday.

The search for the *Dresden* lasted for nearly three months after the withdrawal of the *Inflexible*, occupying a number of British and Allied warships which were needed elsewhere. Otherwise Lüdecke did little damage to the Allied cause; he did not come from the same corsair stable as von Müller. For both the crux was coal, but, whereas the *Emden*'s captain was determined to find it in the holds of the Allies' colliers, the *Dresden*'s waited for German agents to send it in neutral bottoms—and waited in vain. He should not, however, be denied the credit of refusing the suggestion of the German consul at Punta Arenas that he should allow his ship to be interned. He chose instead to hide in lonely Hewett Bay until 26th December when, believing the *Dresden* might be reported by a small schooner that chanced to enter the bay, he thought it wise to move to a more secluded anchorage in Weihnacht Bay. There he was joined on 19th January by the supply ship *Sierra Cordoba*, which had escaped capture by the *Carnarvon* on 26th December by the fortuitous chance that, when sighted, she was within territorial waters under observation by a Chilean destroyer which Stoddart supposed would ensure that she did not engage in any unneutral activity. But Lüdecke did not consider the coal carried by the *Sierra Cordoba* to be sufficient to allow the *Dresden* to wage cruiser warfare. He thought he should wait for at least one of the neutral colliers which he knew German agents were trying to send to him. Unfortunately, although the *Gladstone, Josephina, Eleana Woermann, Bangor* and *Gottia* were all sailed for this purpose, a mutiny broke out onboard the first when she called at Pernambuco, the second was captured off the Falkland Islands by the *Carnarvon* on 6th January, the third was sunk by the *Australia* in the same area, and the last two left Baltimore and Buenos Aires too late to be of service.

On 21st January Berlin signalled to the effect that the *Dresden* should try to return to Germany by 'the sailing vessel route', a freighter having achieved this feat in November. Lüdecke rejected this for five reasons, the two most important being the uncertainty of obtaining coal in the Atlantic and the poor condition of his ship's engines which could no longer be driven at the high speed required to run the gauntlet of the Grand Fleet's blockade of the North Sea. He told Berlin he would 'try to break through to west coast of South America on 3rd February. Intend to carry on commerce warfare in East Indies if sufficient coal is procurable. . . .' a possibility Fisher had feared as early as 6th January when in a characteristic minute to Oliver he wrote: 'If the *Dresden* gets to the Bay of Bengal by means of colliers arranged with Berlin, we shall owe a lot to Sturdee.' But on 10th February Berlin had to tell Lüdecke: 'Further coal supplies for Pacific and Indian Oceans are impossible', and again advised him to return home by way of the Atlantic where a collier would meet him near the equator. Lüdecke was not, however, willing to attempt this; realising that there was a limit to the time his ship could hope to escape discovery by one of the British cruisers he knew to be searching around Tierra del Fuego, he decided to put his own plan into effect. On the 14th February, the *Dresden* and *Sierra Cordoba* sailed in a violent snowstorm, and reached the open sea where they set a northerly course some 200 miles off the west coast of Chile. And on the 19th they reached an area some 200 miles south of Juan Fernandez, which Lüdecke hoped would prove a profitable one. But in three weeks he sighted only one British sailing vessel, the *Conway Castle*, which he sent to the bottom with 2,400 tons of barley intended for Australia. During this time, having taken the last of the *Sierra Cordoba*'s coal, he sent her into Valparaiso on 3rd March from where she was allowed to sail again after embarking 1,200 tons, supposedly for Callao. But she was not to have a chance to transfer any of this to the *Dresden*, for on the 8th Lüdecke's long hunted ship was sighted by the *Kent*.

Lüdecke had been fortunate in eluding discovery much earlier. On 14th December, when it was learned that the *Dresden* had left Punta Arenas, Phillimore believed she must have gone into the Pacific. So the *Inflexible*, *Glasgow* and *Bristol* made a fruitless search of the Chilean coast as far north as Puerto Montt. A search of Tierra del Fuego was not begun until the *Carnarvon* and *Cornwall* returned from investigating the east coast of South America southwards from Port Madryn in accordance with Sturdee's orders. Since the *Kent* and *Orama* had already been sent to the Juan Fernandez area in the Pacific by Admiralty orders, Stoddart, on assuming responsibility for the search, could only despatch the *Cornwall* to search around Cape Horn whilst his own flagship looked for the enemy in the maze of channels and inlets in the Magellan Straits—when as already mentioned she sighted the *Sierra Cordoba* on 26th December, but just missed the *Dresden*. After that, however, Stoddart was joined by the *Glasgow* and *Bristol*, and since he was fairly sure that the *Dresden* was in hiding in this area, he began a systematic search which might well have been successful early in January; for on the 2nd Milward learned that the *Dresden* and her tender were anchored in Weihnacht Bay. Milward at once signalled this news to the Admiralty and Stoddart, but both discredited it: knowing the consul's German business connections, they suspected a plant intended to entice our ships into uncharted waters where they might easily be wrecked.

When the *Carnarvon* had to return to the Falklands to coal on 9th January Stoddart was a baffled man. A full month had passed since the Falklands battle and his search of the Magellan Straits, whose entrances he had left guarded on the east by the *Glasgow* and the west by the *Bristol*, had failed to find the *Dresden*. He had, moreover, obtained no news of her whereabouts that he was willing to believe. He had always to bear in mind that the A.M.C. *Prinz Eitel Friedrich* was somewhere at large, presumably in the Pacific, though he had no more recent news of her than of the *Dresden*. And now he heard that the *Kronprinz Wilhelm* was dangerously active in the Pernambuco focal area which had been left without a regular patrol since the concentration against von Spee. To meet this threat Stoddart sent the *Glasgow* north to Montevideo, whilst the Admiralty ordered him to send the *Cornwall* to St Helena against the possibility that either this A.M.C. or the phantom *Karlsrühe* would appear off German South-West Africa. But despite this reduction in his force, and the risk inherent in leaving only the *Otranto* to guard the Falkland Islands, Stoddart paid a visit to Punta Arenas in the middle of January, and was sufficiently convinced by Milward of the *Dresden*'s continued presence in the area to institute a further search by his flagship and the *Bristol*. It was all but successful; a tug chartered to assist in examining the more hazardous passages penetrated nearly as far as the German cruiser's anchorage; and early one morning the *Carnarvon* passed but did not stop to examine a small steamer that was taking provisions to the *Sierra Cordoba*.

Stoddart's second search of the Magellan Straits having failed, he turned elsewhere, taking the *Carnarvon*, *Bristol* and *Otranto* up the east coast of South America as far as the Abrolhos Rocks (where, on 22nd February the flagship struck an uncharted rock and had to be beached to avoid sinking, until temporary repairs could be effected) whilst the *Glasgow* was ordered south to cover the Straits and the Falklands. Though Milward then told Luce that provisions were still being sent from Punta Arenas to the *Dresden* so that she must be in the area, the *Glasgow*'s captain did not feel justified in hazarding his ship on yet another systematic search. The British task was complicated by the deliberately false reports spread by the Germans in Patagonia, of which one reached the Admiralty about 10th February, to the effect that the *Dresden* was in Last Hope Inlet, the remotest recess of the maze of fiords spreading northwards from Smyth's Channel. And although this rumour was highly unlikely—or perhaps *because* it was so unlikely—the Admiralty decided to act on it: the *Glasgow* was instructed to carry out an immediate search, and both the *Kent* and *Orama* to come south and assist. Two days later Stoddart was ordered to add the *Bristol* to Luce's force. In vain did Milward protest that it was all a German ruse to get our ships out of the way. Indeed, it was not only successful in drawing off the only four British ships in the area whilst the *Dresden* left her hiding place for the Pacific, but resulted in one, the *Bristol*, seriously damaging her rudder on an uncharted shoal so that she had to go into dry dock. But in another respect the ruse was the reverse of successful: on failing to find the *Dresden* in Last Hope, Luce decided that Milward's information was better than the Admiralty was willing to believe, and acted on a report that the *Dresden* had been sighted on 14th February, with the result that the *Galileo*, a small steamer chartered to assist the *Glasgow* and *Kent*, penetrated Weihnacht Bay at the beginning of March. This was, admittedly, a fortnight too late to be of use, but it was much nearer the mark than the Admiralty who, on 4th March, again chose to believe a rumour, once again strongly discounted by Milward, to the effect that the *Dresden* was in Last Hope, and ordered Luce to search this unlikely place for a second time—a clear case of the danger inherent in a distant authority supposing that it should exercise control of operations instead of leaving them to the man on the spot.

By this date half a dozen British cruisers had been carrying out this frustrating form of hide-and-seek for three months. It might have continued for another three but for the chance that the Admiralty received a German telegram from an agent in Chile which, when deciphered in Room 40 O.B., was found to contain orders to a collier to rendezvous with the *Dresden* in a position 300 miles west of Coronel on 5th March. Though it was not believed to be sufficiently authentic to justify calling off Luce's search of Last Hope, the *Kent* was ordered north to investigate. Unfortunately Allen could not arrive on the *Dresden*'s hunting ground until 7th March when he saw nothing. Was he too late? Next morning fog veiled the scene; but it cleared in the afternoon to reveal, not the collier but—at long last—the *Dresden* some 12 miles to the west. The *Kent* immediately gave chase but, though she worked up to 21 knots, Lüdecke was able to prevent her from closing to within gun-range. 'By 2000 [the *Dresden*] was hull down [Allen wrote] and only her masts and the tops of her funnels showed. Our funnels were glowing red hot and the sparks were flying astern. . . . At 2100 it was nearly an hour since I had seen anything'—and it was dark. The *Kent* was also short of coal, so a disappointed Allen returned to the rendezvous where he was at last able to wireless a report of his encounter through the *Dresden*'s jamming. A couple of days later he heard that he had been made a C.B. for his part in the Falklands battle; but 'I did not feel any particular pleasure as our failure to catch the *Dresden* was too recent. I would rather have sunk her than have every honour there is.' Luce received Allen's report that evening, but could not safely leave the fiords of Smyth's Channel until daylight next morning.

Then he sent the *Orama* to bring his colliers up to Vallenar Roads and hurried north to join Allen, who was thus enabled to take the *Kent* into Coronel for coal. The *Orama* rejoined on the 13th and the *Glasgow*'s captain decided to seek his quarry at Mas a Fuera; but before the two ships could take their departure for this western outpost of the Juan Fernandez group, Luce received a report that another collier had been ordered to meet the *Dresden* at the main island, Mas a Tierra. He immediately wirelessed the *Kent* to join him in making a raid on this sparsely inhabited spot next morning.

Lüdecke had eluded a more powerfully armed ship but, since the collier had failed to keep the rendezvous on the 5th, his fuel position was too precarious for him to risk a further chase, even supposing his ship's engines and boilers, now sorely in need of refit, would stand the strain. During the night of 8th March he headed for Mas a Tierra where the *Dresden* anchored in Cumberland Bay a quarter of a mile from the shore at 0800 on the 9th. The Chilean governor boarded her and informed Lüdecke that he must leave within 24 hours, but the German captain pleaded that he could not comply unless he obtained coal since his ship had less than 100 tons remaining in her bunkers. That night the *Dresden* received her last signal: 'His Majesty the Kaiser leaves it to your discretion to lay up [i.e. accept internment].' For Lüdecke this was enough; deciding that he had no practicable alternative, he informed the governor next morning that he would await the arrival of a Chilean warship. Until then, however, he refused to allow the *Dresden*'s engines to be immobilised; but on the 12th he sent four of his officers in a sailing vessel to Valparaiso so that they would escape internment.

At daylight on 14th March the *Glasgow* and *Orama* approached from the west, whilst the *Kent* came in from the east, and found the *Dresden* anchored close under Cumberland Bay's precipitous cliffs. Luce, who had had to flee from von Spee's squadron at Coronel, whose proper decision to engage the *Leipzig* at the Falklands battle had allowed the *Dresden* to escape and involve him in a tedious three months' search for her, did not hesitate over the niceties of International Law. The Admiralty had, after all, signalled: 'Object is destruction not internment.' And, in the absence of a Chilean warship, the local authorities clearly had no means of enforcing the neutrality of this remote island; they had been unable to prevent the *Dresden* exceeding a stay of 24 hours, and they had failed to intern her since she still flew the German ensign. Closing to 8,400 yards, waiting only until the houses of the settlement were out of the line of fire, the *Glasgow* opened fire at 0850, her first two salvoes scoring hits. The *Dresden* could have surrendered honourably then, if not before; but that was not the German tradition. As the *Kent* joined the action, Lüdecke's ship returned her opponents' fire, but, being anchored, she was at such a tactical disadvantage that within three minutes she had suffered enough damage for Lüdecke to hoist a white flag. Seeing this, and the German crew abandoning ship, Luce ordered 'Cease fire' and awaited the arrival of a boat from the *Dresden* flying a flag of truce. There are two versions of what took place when Lieutenant Canaris boarded the *Glasgow*. According to the German, Canaris protested that his ship was in neutral waters and that she was prevented from leaving by damaged engines, to which Luce replied that he had orders to destroy the *Dresden* wherever she might be found, and that questions of International Law could be considered later by the governments concerned; he concluded by asking whether the *Dresden* had struck her flag, to which Canaris responded by indicating that it was still flying at the fore. The British record states, on the other hand, that Canaris protested against the attack on the grounds that the *Dresden* had already been interned, which Luce pointed out was palpably untrue, and that he required unconditional surrender before he was willing to negotiate.

The accuracy of either version is, however, of small importance. Lüdecke had sent Canaris to parley with only one object: he could not honourably allow his ship to fall into British hands, yet he wanted to prevent further useless loss of life among his crew. He had to gain the time needed to prepare her for scuttling so effectively that she could not be salvaged from the shallow waters of the bay: opening her sea cocks, condensers and torpedo tube doors would not be enough. Whilst Luce was apologising to the Chilean governor for inadvertently firing on his boat and offering to pay full compensation for damage done to local property, Lüdecke followed the last of his officers and men towards the shore. And at 1045 the thunder of the *Dresden*'s forward magazine exploding echoed round the cliffs. The British cruisers, wrote Allen, 'closed to within a mile and watched: at first she sank very slowly, going down by the bows. Then more quickly she listed over and sank. The ship's company were fallen in on shore and, as the ship went down, they cheered. Our crews cheered too. It was an extraordinarily interesting sight, the sinking ship with the ensign and the white flag together, the Germans on shore and our decks crowded with men.'

The *Dresden* had suffered eight killed and 16 wounded. For lack of any hospital facilities ashore, Luce chivalrously sent the latter to

Valparaiso in the *Orama* without asking for their internment. Then, as soon as he had settled all claims for compensation by the payment of £500 in gold, the *Glasgow* and *Kent* sailed on 20th March, leaving the Juan Fernandez group of islands, one time home of Alexander Selkirk, to the age-long loneliness from which they had been so rudely awakened by the limitless spread of the war. Lüdecke and the rest of his officers and men had to await the arrival of a Chilean warship which took them to the tedium of internment on Quiriquina Island, whence in time a number managed to escape, the first to do so being Lieutenant Canaris (who reached the rank of admiral in the Navy of the Third Reich, and was head of German Intelligence in the Second World War). Chile, as was to be expected, protested to both British and German Governments at the violation of the sovereignty of their territorial waters. The British quickly pointed out that, because the *Dresden* had so frequently violated Chilean neutrality with impunity (notably by remaining in territorial waters for periods far longer than the authorised 24 hours) they had recently served notice that, if she sought to escape by taking refuge anywhere on the Chilean coast where the authorities had no means of detaining her, then their cruisers would have to invoke the accepted principle of 'hot chase' and sink her themselves. The British note added that, although their minister in Santiago had been given to understand that the Chilean Government had accepted this doctrine, it was greatly regretted that circumstances should have required Captain Luce to act as he did. This prompt apology, which was as quickly accepted, did much to improve Britain's relations with Chile, more especially when the German Government ignored the note sent to them and required von Erckerdt to make a vigorous but evidently pointless protest at the Chileans allowing their neutrality to be abused by Luce's ships. Luce himself was not troubled by all this: he, whose ship had fought at both Coronel and Falklands, had had the ultimate satisfaction of being in at the death, albeit an inglorious one, of the last of von Spee's once victorious squadron.

This, however, is not quite the end of the story of an admiral whose name must be an honoured one in German annals: 20 years later a phoenix was to rise from the ashes. In the 1930s a renascent German Navy was notably strengthened by three hybrid vessels known to the world as pocket battleships. Displacing more than 12,000 tons, they were as large as the Third Reich dared build without transparently exceeding the limit imposed by the Treaty of Versailles. Armed with six 11-inch guns mounted in two triple turrets and provided with a measure of armour protection, these ships were intended to be more than a match for any cruiser afloat; and their speed of 26 knots exceeded that of all but a few of the world's capital ships. The first was christened *Deutschland*; the others bore the name of the German commanders at the battles of Jutland and Coronel.

In 1939 Germany had no reason for stationing warships overseas, but one lesson of the First World War had not been lost on her Navy's Commander-in-Chief. A surface fleet in the North Sea had been unable to destroy Britain's command of the sea, but a U-boat campaign against her maritime trade had brought the country within six weeks of starvation. So Admiral Raeder reasoned that some of Germany's surface ships would be best employed in support of her limited number of U-boats, carrying out cruiser warfare after the pattern set by the *Emden* in 1914. In the middle of August, 1939, he sent the *Deutschland* and the *Admiral Graf Spee* out into the Atlantic, where they were poised ready to strike when Britain was obliged to declare war on 3rd September. The *Deutschland*, operating in the North Atlantic, sank two ships before she was recalled to Germany on 1st November. Captain Langsdorff of the *Graf Spee* had more success: operating in the South Atlantic and in the Indian Ocean, he sank nine ships, totalling 50,000 tons, treating their crews with a courtesy reminiscent of von Müller of the *Emden*.

But the British Navy had also learned much from the First World War and in the subsequent two decades of peace. There was no hesitation, no half-hearted measures, this time in dealing with the threat presented by another Graf von Spee, once it was known that the marauder was at large. The Admiralty, again headed by the indomitable Churchill, with a First Sea Lord, Admiral Sir Dudley Pound, who had been an instructor to the first staff course at the old War College, and a properly recognised Naval Staff of officers trained at the Naval Staff College, quickly deployed eight groups of capital ships, aircraft carriers and cruisers, provided by France as well as Britain, to hunt Langsdorff down. One group went to the Plate, as in 1914 a focal area for maritime trade, and here at dawn on 13th December, almost 25 years to the day after von Spee's death, the *Graf Spee* was sighted by the British cruisers *Ajax*, Captain C. H. L. Woodhouse, flying the broad pendant of Commodore H. Harwood, *Achilles*, Captain W. E. Parry, of the New Zealand Navy, both armed with eight 6-inch guns, and

Exeter, Captain F. S. Bell, with six 8-inch guns. Unlike Cradock's armoured cruisers, all were modern vessels that had been some time in commission. Like Sturdee, however, Harwood had all day before him; he had, too, the advantage of speed and numbers; on the other hand, he faced an enemy vessel potentially more powerful than any of his own squadron.

He solved the problem by dividing his force; whilst the *Exeter* moved in to attack the *Graf Spee* from one bearing, the *Ajax* and *Achilles* threatened her from another. After making the initial mistake of dividing his armament, Langsdorff concentrated on dealing with the most powerful of the British ships, and by 0730 he had so damaged the *Exeter* that she had to withdraw from the battle. The German captain then turned his attention to the *Ajax* and *Achilles* whose pugnacious tactics prevented him sinking the crippled *Exeter*. Had Langsdorff steered east it is possible that he might have kept them at bay until he could escape under cover of darkness; but he was unwilling to accept this risk against a squadron that had proved its superior tactical ability and training; he steered for the safety of the neutral port of Montevideo, which Harwood's two small cruisers could not prevent the *Graf Spee* entering that night.

Langsdorff obtained a 72-hour extension of the permissible 24 hours stay to repair his ship's damage; then he had to sail. Harwood, patiently awaiting him, had been reinforced only by the cruiser *Cumberland*, armed with eight 8-inch guns. But in Montevideo Langsdorff had heard that the aircraft-carrier *Ark Royal* and the battle-cruiser *Renown* were also there; and though this intelligence might not be confirmed (these two ships, which had been ordered to the Plate, actually arrived at Rio de Janeiro on 17th December to fuel), the German captain must surely have remembered how von Spee had been trapped by the *Invincible* and *Inflexible*. He might, none the less, have risked action despite the example set by Lüdecke of the *Dresden*, if Hitler, unwilling to suffer the ignominy of having one of his pocket battleships sunk at sea, had not ordered Langsdorff to scuttle his ship. Langsdorff complied in the Plate estuary on the evening of 17th December, within sight of Harwood's watching cruisers, then returned to Montevideo to efface this shameful act by committing suicide. In Churchill's words: 'In this sombre dark winter . . . the brilliant action of the Plate . . . came like a flash of light and colour on the scene, carrying with it an encouragement to all who are fighting—to ourselves and to our Allies.'

That the ship destroyed in December 1939 should have borne the name of the German admiral whose squadron was all but annihilated in the same ocean area in December, 1914, was a curious coincidence. But there are more interesting parallels between the battle of the Plate and the battle of the Falklands. But the most significant, never, one hopes, to be lost on those responsible for our country's defence, is that in two world wars, Britain's first important naval victory was gained half the world away in protection of our maritime trade:

> *Her island-myriads fed from alien hands—*
> *The fleet of England is her all-in-all;*
> *Her fleet is in your hands*
>   *And in her fleet her Fate.*

APPENDIX I: THE SHIPS AND THEIR CAPTAINS

Ship	Type	Year of Completion	Displacement (in tons)	Guns (with maximum range in yds.)	Speed (in knots*)	Principal Armour	Commanded by	Complement
BRITISH *Canopus*	Battle-ship	1899	12,950	4—12" (13,500) 12—6" (10,000)	18	6" belt 12" barbettes 8" turrets	Captain H. S. Grant	750
Inflexible	Battle-cruisers	1908	17,250	8—12" (16,400) 16— 4"	25	6" belt 7" barbettes 7" turrets	Captain R. F. Phillimore	780
Invincible							Captain P. T. H. Beamish. *Flagship of Vice-Admiral Sir Doveton Sturdee*	780
Carnarvon	Armoured Cruiser	1904	10,850	4—7.5" (12,000) 6—6" (11,200)	22	6" belt 6" barbettes 5" turrets	Captain H. I. d'E. Skipwith. *Flagship of Rear-Admiral A. P. Stoddart*	650
Cornwall	Armoured Cruisers	1903	9,800	14—6" (11,200)	23	4" belt 5" barbettes 5" turrets	Captain W. M. Ellerton	675
Kent							Captain J. D. Allen	675
Monmouth							Captain F. Brandt	675
Defence	Armoured Cruiser	1908	14,600	4—9.2" (12,500) 10—7.5" (12,500)	23	6" belt 7" barbettes 6—8" turrets	Captain F. Wray	750
Good Hope	Armoured Cruiser	1902	14,100	2—9.2" (12,500) 16—6" (11,200)	23	6" belt 6" barbettes 5" turrets	Captain P. Francklin. *Flagship of Rear-Admiral Sir Christopher Cradock*	900

Ship	Type	Year		Armament	Speed	Protective plating	Captain	
Bristol / *Glasgow*	Light Cruisers	1911	4,800	2—6" (11,200) / 10—4" (9,800)	25	Protective plating	Captain B. H. Fanshawe / Captain J. Luce	375 / 375
Sydney	Light Cruiser	1913	5,600	8—6" (11,200)	26	Protective plating	Captain J. Glossop	375
GERMAN *Gneisenau* / *Scharnhorst*	Armoured Cruisers	1907	11,600	8—8·2" (13,500) / 6—5·9" (11,200)	20	6" belt / 6" barbettes / 7" turrets	Captain Maerker / Captain Schultz *Flagship of Vice-Admiral Graf von Spee*	765 / 765
Dresden	Light Cruiser	1909	3,600	10—4·1" (10,500)	24	Protective plating	Captain Lüdecke	320
Emden	Light Cruiser	1908	3,600	10—4·1" (10,500)	24	Protective plating	Captain von Müller	320
Leipzig	Light Cruiser	1906	3,250	10—4·1" (10,500)	23	Protective plating	Captain Haun	285
Nürnberg	Light Cruiser	1908	3,450	10—4·1" (10,500)	23	Protective plating	Captain von Schönberg	295

* Coal-fired ships could only maintain their designed speed for about eight hours; it was then necessary to clean fires, which involved a temporary reduction in speed, unless a progressive reduction in speed due to clinkered firebars was accepted. As important, the coal supply needed to feed the boilers when steaming at high speed could not be maintained once the bunkers abreast the boiler-rooms had been emptied, unless seamen were taken from their guns, etc., to trim coal from bunkers forward and aft of the boiler-rooms into those abreast them. Designed speed figures for coal-fired ships are therefore to be regarded as relative except for the short duration of a battle. This includes all that took part in the battles of Coronel and the Falklands except for the *Invincible* and *Inflexible* which, though primarily coal-burning, carried a limited amount of oil: they were able to maintain their designed speed for longer.

APPENDIX II: COMMUNICATIONS

For a proper understanding of the events recorded in these pages it should be appreciated that wireless telegraphy had only been introduced into the British and German Navies during the previous decade, that it was subject to serious limitations, and that neither Navy had had previous experience of its use in war.

Direct communication between Whitehall and British ships in South American waters, and between Berlin and German ships in the Pacific was not possible. Signals* from the British Admiralty to ships off the *east* coast of South America were sent by cable to Montevideo whence the Uruguayan Government allowed them to be transmitted by Cerrito wireless station to the Falkland Islands, and from there they were re-transmitted to ships at sea. Similarly, ships in this area passed signals to the Admiralty via Falkland Islands wireless station to Cerrito (or direct to Cerrito) and thence by cable to Whitehall. In both cases signals were subject to delays varying from several hours to two or three days when atmospheric conditions were poor. British ships off the *west* coast of South America were not so fortunate. Communication with the Falkland Islands was seldom possible owing to the intervening Andes mountains and poor atmospheric conditions, and the use of wireless stations in Chile was not practicable because that Government prohibited the transmission and reception of signals in cipher. Signals from the Admiralty to Cradock had, therefore, to be sent by cable to a British consul for collection by one of his ships. For this reason Cradock had to send one into port (e.g. the *Glasgow* on 1st November) at as frequent intervals as possible. This meant that signals between the Admiralty and Cradock were normally liable to be delayed several days and sometimes a week or more.

Communication between the German Admiralty and their ships in the Pacific suffered the same restrictions without, moreover, the advantage of a wireless station of their own similar to the British one in the Falkland Islands (once the high-powered wireless station on Yap, which was in cable communication with Berlin, had been destroyed on 12th August). (Hence, for example, the visit of the *Nürnberg* to Honolulu.) On the other hand, once von Spee had reached South American waters, there were German merchant ships in various harbours where the authorities of countries in sympathy with Germany were not always very particular about the regulations which prohibited the use of wireless by belligerent vessels in neutral ports. So

* The British naval term 'signal' has been used throughout this book for messages sent by radio and cable, although in 1914 the Royal Navy preferred the term 'telegram' for messages exchanged with the Admiralty because they were usually passed by cable or land line over part or whole of their route.

Berlin then had a reasonably effective means of communication with von Spee by cable to one of their consuls for re-transmission by a merchant ship which could, if necessary, put to sea for this purpose; and the same route in reverse was available for von Spee to communicate with Berlin, though he had a greater need to communicate with German authorities in South America to ensure his coal supplies.

Whilst both British and German Navies appreciated the new flexibility which the introduction of wireless gave to naval operations overseas, they had not realised the extent to which it was a two-edged weapon. Arc and spark transmitters splashed across a broad band of the medium frequency spectrum and were easily intercepted by receivers within range that had neither valves nor precision tuning, only crystal or magnetic detectors. A message transmitted from a ship at sea was consequently liable to reveal its presence to the enemy, as also would a ship answering a call by a shore station. Both sides made use of this; though ships were unable to measure wireless bearings, they could distinguish between a British and a German vessel by the note of its transmitter (normally Marconi in the former and Telefunken in the latter) and by the type of message radiated, estimate its range, and sometimes recognise its call-sign. For notwithstanding this danger, few shore wireless stations that could broadcast messages to ships at sea without requiring them to break wireless silence had been provided; and command organisations had not been adjusted to allow for the movements of ships and their supporting supply vessels to be controlled except by the senior officer afloat using his own ship's wireless. (Jerram, Commander-in-Chief China, seems to have been the first to realise that he could command his widely dispersed units better from headquarters ashore than from a sea-going cruiser.)

Thus Cradock risked revealing the presence of his squadron in the days immediately preceding Coronel: the *Good Hope*, the *Canopus* and the *Glasgow*, being separated, all used their wireless. Von Spee, on the other hand, with his squadron concentrated was able to arrange for all messages to be transmitted by one ship, thereby deceiving his adversary into the fatal supposition that only the *Leipzig* was off Coronel. The Germans were just as cautious in using wireless after they had rounded the Horn so that Sturdee knew nothing of their approach to the Falklands. But he had taken similar precautions when the battle-cruisers joined Stoddart's cruisers at the Abrolhos Rocks, arranging for such signals as might have to be sent during the squadron's voyage south to be transmitted by the *Glasgow* or *Bristol* whose presence in the area was already known to the enemy. Thereby he prevented von Spee from learning that British reinforcements had reached the Falkland Islands.

BIBLIOGRAPHY

PUBLISHED WORKS

British

Bingham, Commander The Hon. H., *Falklands, Jutland and the Bight*
Churchill, Winston, *The World Crisis, 1911–18*, Vols. I and II
Cooper, Commander H. Spencer, *The Battle of the Falkland Islands*
Corbett, Sir Julian, *Naval Operations (Official History of the War)*, Vols. I and II
Fayle, C. E., *Seaborne Trade*
Hankey, Lord, *The Supreme Command 1914–18*
Hoehling, A. A., *Lonely Command: the Story of the 'Emden'*
Hirst, Paymaster Commander Lloyd, *Coronel and After*
Irving, J., *Coronel and Falklands*
Jose, A. W., *Official History of Australia in the War of 1914–18*, Vol. IX, The Royal Australian Navy
Marder, A. J., *Fear God and Dread Nought*
Marder, A. J., *Portrait of an Admiral*
Middlemas, Keith, *Command the Far Seas*
Phillips, Keith, *Coronel* (A narrative poem)
Pitt, Barrie, *Coronel and Falklands*
Verner, Commander R., *The Battle-cruisers at the Action off the Falkland Islands*
Wyllie, W. L. and M. F. Wren, *Sea Fights of the Great War*

German

Busch, F. O., *Admiral Graf Spee's Sieg und Untergang*
Dick, Admiral C., *The Cruiser Squadron, its Formation; Victory and End*
Hartz, H. von Waldenar, *Von Tsingtau zu den Falkland Inseln*
Joseph, Franz, Oberleutenant, Prince von Hohenzollern, *Emden* (English translation)
Kirchoff, Vice-Admiral Hermann, *Maximilian Graf von Spee*
Laar, C., *Die Grauen Wölfe des Grafen Spee*
Mücke, Hellmuth von, *Emden-Ayesha*
Pochhammer, Hans, *Before Jutland: Admiral Spee's Last Voyage* (English translation)

BIBLIOGRAPHY

Raeder, E., *Der Krieg zur See, 1914–18, Der Kreuzerkrieg Band I. Der
    Kreuzergeschweden* (The official history)
Schneider, H., *Die Letzte Fahrt des Kleinen Kreuzer 'Dresden'*
Schoen, Walter von, *Kreuzerkrieg führen*
Tirpitz, Grand Admiral von, *My Memoirs* (English translation)

SOURCES PRINTED FOR
OFFICIAL OR PRIVATE CIRCULATION ONLY

Admiralty, *Naval Staff Monographs*, Vol. I (OU. 5413) and Vol. V,
    (OU. 5413C)
Dewar, Vice-Admiral, K.G.B., *The Coronel Campaign*

CONTEMPORARY UNPUBLISHED SOURCES

*The letters, diaries, journals, etc. of the following (ranks given are those held
    at the time):*
Allen, Captain J. D., of H.M.S. *Kent*
Backhouse, Lieutenant-Commander C. L., of H.M.S. *Glasgow*
Begbie, Lieutenant H. H.-G., of H.M.S. *Invincible*
Bethell, Midshipman J. S., of H.M.S. *Cornwall*
Danckwerts, Lieutenant V. H., of H.M.S. *Kent*
Duckworth, Clerk A. D., of H.M.S. *Invincible*
Giffard, Lieutenant-Commander F., of H.M.S. *Invincible*
Goddard, T. N., A.D.C. to the Governor of the Falkland Islands
Hirst, Assistant Paymaster Lloyd, of H.M.S. *Glasgow*
Hordern, Lieutenant-Commander P., of H.M.S. *Canopus*
Leveson, Lieutenant L. I. G., of H.M.S. *Invincible*
Mandley, Midshipman R. H., of H.M.S. *Carnarvon*
Oliver, Sub-Lieutenant R. D., of H.M.S. *Inflexible*
Penney, Midshipman P. J. M., of H.M.S. *Carnarvon*
Start, Engineer Lieutenant-Commander S. P., of H.M.S. *Canopus*
Steele, Clerk R. C., of H.M.S. *Invincible*
Sturdee, Vice-Admiral Sir Doveton, of H.M.S. *Invincible*
Stewart, Sub-Lieutenant R. R., of H.M.S. *Invincible*
Verteuil, Surgeon F. L. De, of H.M.S. *Good Hope*

Index of Persons and Places

The numerals in **heavy type** refer to the figure-numbers of the illustrations

Index of Ships

H.M. SHIPS

GERMAN WARSHIPS

OTHER VESSELS